I0824890

"Like a modern-day version of the beloved *Valley of Vision*, *Sheltering Mercy* is a collection of poems inspired by the Psalms. This small, beautiful book holds timeless reminders of God's enduring promises."

—**Sandra McCracken**, singer-songwriter

"Over the course of my career, I've spent countless hours laboring over vocal harmonies. There's something beautiful about hearing different, complementary (or consonant) notes at the same time. The prayers in *Sheltering Mercy* produce a similar result. They harmonize with the text of Scripture and make it come alive in a whole new way."

—**Michael W. Smith**, singer-songwriter

"Psalm-praying is one of the oldest and most powerful ways of learning to talk to God. Yet the words of the Psalms are distant from us, and Christians are not always sure how to make those ancient words *our* words. Smith and Wilt provide in this book the kindling for our own Psalm-praying, provoking our response and forming the word of God in our mouths. Pray the words of Scripture and then let their words spark your imagination and slow you down enough to learn the grammar of intimacy with God."

—**Glenn Packiam**, author of *The Resilient Pastor* and *Blessed Broken Given*

"This beautiful collection of psalms expressed as poetic prayer reminds us of the relevance of reverence in our daily lives and the hope breathed through even the darkest of sufferings. Alight on a different poem each day, and find rest in its cadence, restoration in its celebration, and guidance from new songs grown from deep-rooted wisdom."

—**Carolyn Weber**, author of *Surprised by Oxford* and *Holy Is the Day*

ENDLESS GRACE

For more Psalm-inspired prayers by
Ryan Whitaker Smith and Dan Wilt,
see SHELTERING MERCY (*Brazos, 2022*).

ENDLESS GRACE

PRAYERS INSPIRED BY THE PSALMS

RYAN WHITAKER SMITH
AND DAN WILT

BrazosPress
a division of Baker Publishing Group
Grand Rapids, Michigan

Published by Brazos Press
a division of Baker Publishing Group
www.brazospress.com

Printed in the United States of America

Library of Congress Cataloging-in-Publication Data

Names: Smith, Ryan Whitaker, 1983– author. | Wilt, Dan, author.
Title: Endless grace : prayers inspired by the Psalms / Ryan Whitaker Smith and Dan Wilt.
Description: Grand Rapids, Michigan : Brazos Press, a division of Baker Publishing Group, [2023] | Includes bibliographical references.
Identifiers: LCCN 2022026449 | ISBN 9781587435478 (cloth) | ISBN 9781493440443 (ebook) | ISBN 9781493440450 (pdf)
Subjects: LCSH: Bible. Psalms, LXXVI-CL—Devotional use. | Prayers.
Classification: LCC BS1430.54 .S5835 2023 | DDC 242/.5—dc23/eng/20220630
LC record available at https://lccn.loc.gov/2022026449

ISBN 978-1-58743-613-0 (boxed set)

Baker Publishing Group publications use paper produced from sustainable forestry practices and post-consumer waste whenever possible.

23 24 25 26 27 28 29 7 6 5 4 3 2 1

For all the beloved of God:
may you find new songs to sing,
new praises to bring,
new grammar to proclaim
the length,
height,
depth,
breadth
of His kindness to us.

CONTENTS

INTRODUCTION

In the first verses of the first chapter of the book of Psalms, we are promised that a blessing awaits those who resolve to *meditate* on the precepts of the Lord (Ps. 1:2). The Hebrew word is *hagah*, which means to *ponder, imagine, mutter, study*. In an age of relentless busyness and nonstop information consumption, the notion of reading anything slowly and contemplatively is novel—but that is precisely what the Psalms (indeed, all of Scripture) invite us to do. To linger. To reflect. To allow the words to shape and form us over time.

We are called to meditate on the written Word of God through the day (Ps. 119:97) and the night (63:6), in the midst of oppression (119:23) and false accusation (119:78), as a means of guarding against temptation (119:9) and resisting anger (4:4)—that we might recall the works of the Lord (77:11–12), approach Him in worshipful reverence (119:48), ponder all His benefits (103:2), and remember His many mercies (25:6).

Endless Grace, like its companion volume, *Sheltering Mercy*, attempts to take that exhortation to heart, approaching the Psalms as literature designed for prayerful meditation. Both volumes emerged from times of private devotion as a means of engaging with Scripture in a thoughtful, creative way. As writers in different fields, our intention was to pray *along with* the Psalms—to respond to their hopes and fears, confessions and frustrations, with the same naked vulnerability with which the psalmists approached their songs of praise and lament.

The result is a collection of free-verse renderings—impressionistic poetry without the limitations of meter or rhyme. Think of these prayers as lyrical sketches of the scriptural landscape where we find ourselves sojourning. While these prayers attempt to follow the structure of the psalm with which they are resonating, they are not paraphrases or translations; rather, they are *prayerful responses*.

In our introduction to *Sheltering Mercy*, we spoke of the unexpected joy of finding that the whole body of Scripture has provided the content for these unapologetically Christocentric prayers. The Bible, after all, tells one overarching story, and Christ is the central figure of the narrative. In the words of C. S. Lewis, "This is one of the rewards of reading the Old Testament regularly. You keep on discovering more and more what a tissue of quotations from it the New Testament is; how constantly Our Lord repeated, reinforced, continued, refined, and sublimated, the Judaic ethics, how very seldom He introduced a novelty."[1]

1. C. S. Lewis, *Reflections on the Psalms* (1958; repr., San Francisco: HarperCollins, 2017), 30–31.

While these prayers are intended to be used primarily for personal devotion, we have heard stories of them finding their way into worship services, Bible studies, small groups, hospital rooms, nursing homes. As it turns out, there is not just one way to engage with these prayers. Read them in solitude, in company, at home, in a waiting room, from a stage, in whole or in part, in silence or in song.

However this book finds its way to you, and however you choose to interact with it, our hope is that you would encounter Christ in its pages and meditate, along with us, on His sheltering mercy and endless grace.

PSALM 76

YOUR NEW WORLD

Father God,
in Your mercy
You have chosen[1]
a People,
a Family,
a Church—
that we might bear Your name
as citizens of heaven,[2]
children of New Creation.[3]

You have made Your home with us,
ushering us into the household of God—
to a kingdom unmoved and unshaken,[4]
to a feast unending.

You have triumphed over the grave,[5]
lifting us from deep darkness
to walk in Your everlasting light.

All instruments of death—
all that draws blood,
robs life,
steals innocence—
will be disarmed,
dismantled,
beat into shovels
and hoes
to till the soil of Your New World.[6]

Your peace is stronger than violence;
Your mercy fiercer than judgment.

1. 1 Pet. 2:9. 2. Phil. 3:20. 3. Eph. 2:19–22. 4. Heb. 12:28. 5. Rom. 6:8–10. 6. Isa. 2:4.

All who stand against You—
godless forces,
seething and swarming on the horizon—
will buckle at the knees,
falling prostrate
before the Judge of all the earth.

Strength will seep from them.
Paralyzing fear will grip them.
Breath will escape from them.

They will see,
with startling clarity,
He whom they have opposed—
and their hearts will wither.

Listen!
as all lands and seas,
fish and fowl,
and all manner of God-breathed things
hold their breath,
as the King rises in power,
a sword of justice in His fist—
to put an end to evil,
banish suffering,
make a new beginning
for the children of His covenant.

In that day,
will Your enemies not bow?
Will those who have cursed You
not confess Your lordship?[7]

As for me,
I will remain steadfast:
Daily kneeling.

7. Rom. 14:11.

Daily confessing.
Daily proclaiming—
for there is none like You[8]
in heaven or on earth:
a God so awesome in power,[9]
so approachable in intimacy,
so lavish in love.[10]

Amen.

8. Ps. 86:8. 9. Ps. 68:35. 10. Exod. 34:6.

PSALM 77

I REMEMBER

Father,
there are times when I fear
my voice[1] is not
loud enough,
bold enough,
true enough
to be heard by You,
the God Who Listens.[2]

Though I have courage,
faith,[3]
breath,[4]
intention—
joy escapes me.

In its absence
I am weak[5]—
heart-heavy,[6]
soul-starved—
yearning for a peace
only You can bring.

Restless,
I labor through the night,
pricked in spirit,
plagued by worry.[7]

In these long hours,
this insufferable silence,
I lose sight of all that is

1. Ps. 5:3. 2. 1 John 5:15. 3. Heb. 11:1. 4. Job 33:4. 5. Rom. 8:26.
6. Ps. 34:18. 7. Ps. 63:6–8.

good
and beautiful
and true.[8]

No comfort comes.
No solace descends.

Like You,
I am,
for the moment,
speechless.

Memories haunt me:
spectral visions of past consolations,
as evasive as the peace that eludes me.

I dig in the dirt,
searching for some forgotten truth
buried in sod and stone.

Once,
when I was weak,
did You not feed me with Your Word?[9]
When my love was cold,
my desires disordered,[10]
did You not brood over the chaos of my life?[11]

I cling to faith:
a tenuous thread.

Have You forgotten me?
Have Your mercies come to an end?
Your promises come to nothing?

Who am I
to make demands of You?
To call You to account?

8. Phil. 4:8. 9. Ps. 119:50. 10. Inspired by Augustine, *Confessions* 4.10.15.
11. Gen. 1:1–2.

Remember,
O my soul,
the glory of the Lord.
That which I have seen,
I will see again.

I will walk once more
in the favor of God,
the blessing of God,
the power of God.

Who is like You, Lord?
Holy.
True.
Light undiminished.
Grace unabridged.

My heart was a locked room,
but You found Your way in.
I have touched Your scars,
seen Your face.[12]

Will I not see You again?

Remember,
O my soul,
the glory of the Lord.

Your power shakes mountains.[13]
Parts seas.[14]
Cuts covenants.[15]
Makes a way.[16]

At Your coming,[17]
oceans rush
and roar,

12. John 20:26–28. 13. Exod. 19:18. 14. Exod. 14:21–31. 15. Gen. 15:17. 16. Isa. 43:16–19. 17. Ps. 104:3.

skies bellow,
clouds spill rain;
all creation groans.[18]

And so I wait,
as covenant people do—
for a cloud by day,[19]
fire by night:[20]
the leading of Your Spirit.

Amen.

18. Rom. 8:22–25. 19. Neh. 9:12. 20. Exod. 13:21.

PSALM 78

SANCTIFIED MEMORY

Father,
grant me a sanctified memory
to recall the things You have done
in the midst of human history—
things hidden from the foundation of the world,[1]
made manifest in the fullness of time.[2]

May I,
with holy hindsight,
be one with all the saints before me,
as I tell Your story
again
and again—
that godly wisdom
be passed down,
generation
to generation.

In faithfulness,
You led the nation of Israel,
writing Your law upon their hearts,[3]
setting before them Life and Death,[4]
that they might flourish
in the land of their possession,
turning from the wickedness of their forebears—
from those who walked in defiance of Your truth,
who mocked Your wisdom.

May my heart be steadfast, O God.

1. 1 Sam. 2:8. 2. Gal. 4:4–7. 3. Jer. 31:33; Heb. 8:10–12; 10:16. 4. Deut. 30:15–16.

Do not let me be like those who see
but do not believe;
who witness
but do not profess.

Your glory was displayed before them!
They saw seas parted,[5]
Your presence in cloud and fire,[6]
water drawn from stone . . .[7]
but it was not enough.

They became bitter.
Resentful.
Unimpressed.
Unsatisfied.

You gave them food from heaven,[8]
opened streams in the wilderness,
provided for their every need—
and still they questioned Your goodness.

In the face of such faithlessness,
Your anger burned against them.[9]

As for me,
may I be steadfast, O God.

Like them,
I have fallen prey to apathy and indifference—
though You have moved heaven and earth
to save me,
clothe me,
feed me—
my life sustained by Your active grace,
Your intentional kindness,
Your sheltering mercy.

5. Exod. 14:21–22. 6. Exod. 13:21. 7. Exod. 17:1–6. 8. Exod. 16:11–35. 9. Num. 11:1–3.

All I have needed
You have provided:[10]
Breath.
Bread.
Light.
Laughter.

Creation is Your kindness, externalized.

Despite Your providence,
I have courted resentment,
fostered discontent.
Was it not for this reason
that You struck down those who scorned You?

Forgive me, Lord.

Still, they did not relent.
Their pride made fools of them—
made them blind to Your providence,
deaf to Your grace.

They invited destruction upon themselves.

Like them,
I have repented,[11]
sought Your face,[12]
returned to Your mercy.

Like them,
my prayers were often empty words—
my promises hollow,
my faith spineless.

But in my faithlessness,
You have remained faithful.[13]

10. Inspired by a line in the hymn "Great Is Thy Faithfulness" (1923) by Thomas O. Chisholm. 11. Mark 1:15. 12. Ps. 27:8. 13. Ps. 89:8.

In my brokenness,
Your blood has covered me.
You have grace for my fallenness,
mercy for my weakness.

Like all wayward saints before me,
I have wandered in desolate places,
choosing lostness over foundness,
drifting over belonging.

Have mercy on me, Lord.

If Your people could forget
their deliverance from Egypt,
when Your power was seen
in undeniable displays of glory—
all creation at Your command
as You rendered judgment over Your enemies—
miracles
and wonders,
plagues
and terrors—
then I, too,
am capable of forgetting
all You have done for me.

How often have You guided me to safety?
How often have You rescued me from ruin?

Your grace has made a way for me:
it has parted seas,
carved a path through the wilderness,
led me to a land of abundance,
to the mountain of Your presence.

But I have been reckless with Your mercy,
callous with Your commandments.

I have run after lesser gods,
driven by the lusts of the flesh and eye,
by the pride of life.[14]

While judgment once fell upon the disobedient—
curses
and captivity,
death
and darkness,
the consequences of their rebellion—
Your cross has spoken life over me.[15]
In Your mercy,
You have shouldered the weight of my sin,
borne my griefs
and sorrows,[16]
ransomed me from ruin.

Have You not chosen the low things of the world—
the meek,
the forsaken,
the despised[17]—
to bring about Your purposes?

You humble the proud,
exalt the humble[18]—
for You are
Lord of the Lowly.[19]
Defender of the Downcast.[20]
King of the Contrite[21]—
for theirs is the kingdom of heaven.[22]

Grant me a sanctified memory, Lord,
that I might not forget Your abundant mercies.

Amen.

14. 1 John 2:16. 15. Heb. 12:22–24. 16. Isa. 53:4. 17. 1 Cor. 1:27–31. 18. Luke 18:14. 19. Matt. 11:29. 20. Ps. 43:5. 21. Isa. 57:15. 22. Matt. 5:3.

PSALM 79

TABLE OF MERCY

Lord God,
we have opened our
hearts,
minds,
bodies,
temples,
to the influence of idols.

Have mercy on us.[1]

We have allowed
twisted intentions,
wayward wants,
destructive desires
a place at the table of mercy.[2]

Have mercy on us.

We have followed the spirit of the age:
amused,
allured,
coerced,
conformed.

Have mercy on us.

We have courted death,
wooed destruction,
offered ourselves up as lambs for slaughter.

Have mercy on us.

1. Inspired by the Jesus Prayer of liturgical tradition. 2. Luke 24:30.

Once we walked in victory,
but now we are lifeless:
possessing a form of godliness,
but denying its power.[3]

We are pitied,
parodied,
skewered,
scorned.

Have mercy on us.

In the midst of judgment,
is there hope for restoration?
Occasion for mercy?

Destroy that which destroys us, Lord.
Break that which breaks us.
Restore our communion—
the bread and the cup[4]
at the table of mercy.

For not one of us is without sin.[5]

Save us, O Lord,
from the sway of lesser loves.
May peace triumph over violence,
mercy over judgment.[6]

Forgive what we have been.
Sanctify what we are.
Order what we shall be.[7]

By the blood of the Lamb,
remember our sins no more.[8]

3. 2 Tim. 3:5. 4. 1 Cor. 11:23–26. 5. Rom. 3:22–24. 6. James 2:13. 7. From a historic prayer in the liturgical tradition. 8. Heb. 8:12.

We are a temple, desecrated;
a holy place in ruins,
haunted by the cries of the innocent.

Evil spreads its sickness
through every vine
and vein,
until every field
is a field of blood;
every valley
a Gehenna.

But nothing is hidden from You.[9]
All will come to light.

When You restore us,
when Your Spirit breathes
life into these bones,[10]
the nations will cry to You,
the seat of their desire,[11]
and the temple of the earth
will be set free from its bondage
into the freedom of the glory
of the children of God.[12]

The prayers of the saints
are poured out before You:
a fragrant incense[13]
rising to Your throne.

Hear the cries of the righteous, Lord.

May those who turn their face against You,
who shun Your mercy,
defy Your way,
deride the children of Your covenant,

9. Luke 8:17. 10. Ezek. 37:1–14. 11. Hag. 2:7. 12. Rom. 8:21. 13. Rev. 5:8.

reap what they have sown—
while the heirs of Your promise[14]
venture deeper
and deeper
into the love of God,
ever praising You
for Your sustaining hand,[15]
Your endless grace.

Yes, Lord,
we gather once again
at the table of mercy
to tell what You have done.[16]

Amen.

14. Gal. 4:28. 15. Heb. 1:3. 16. Ps. 71:15.

PSALM 80

THE SEED OF YOUR PLANTING

Father God:
Defender.[1]
Guardian.
King of the Cosmos.
Lord of Heavenly Lights[2]—
Hear my prayer today.

Do not withhold Your goodness from me.[3]
Illumine this darkness,
that Your power and glory
might fall upon me once again.

Rebuild me.
Renew me.
Be gracious to me.
Shine upon me.
Give me peace.[4]

Once I walked in Your joy,
but now I am saddled with grief.
My prayers are empty words,
my songs, tuneless drivel.
For reasons unknown,
I suffer Your silence.

Rebuild me.
Renew me.
Be gracious to me.

1. Ps. 68:5. 2. James 1:17. 3. Ps. 84:11. 4. Num. 6:24–26.

Shine upon me.
Give me peace.

When I was a slave to sin,
You liberated me.[5]
When I was oppressed by darkness,
You drew me to Your glorious light.[6]

I was a dormant seed,
but You planted me in fertile soil:
watered me,
nurtured me,
that I might become a thriving, flourishing thing—
a towering oak
in an arid wasteland.

But now I am sapped of strength,
stripped of glory,
a cursed stalk
withering by the roadside.[7]

In my suffering,[8]
remember me, Lord;
remember who I am to You:
seed of Your planting,[9]
child of Your grace.[10]

May this howling darkness
know the fierceness of Your light.
At Your Word,
may these devils flee![11]

Let me know the touch of Your hand once again,
the steadying warmth of Your presence.
In crippling weakness,
be my strength.[12]

5. Rom. 6:5–6. 6. 1 Pet. 2:9. 7. Matt. 13:20–21. 8. John 12:24. 9. Matt. 13:23. 10. 2 Tim. 2:1. 11. Matt. 4:1–11. 12. Exod. 15:2.

Rebuild me.
Renew me.
Be gracious to me.
Shine upon me.
Give me peace.

PSALM 81

WELLSPRING OF PRAISE

Lord God,
my heart is a wellspring of praise.[1]
Awed by Your glory,
humbled by Your goodness,
songs pour out of me:
endless hallelujahs!

Worship is remembrance:
sacred recollection
of Your power,
providence,
presence,
peace.

While the world busies itself with passing things,[2]
I will bless You
on this Remembering Day—
for You guide me on the path of life:[3]
in victory,
defeat,
toil,
rest.

Once I stood on the outskirts of Eden,
barred from the promises of God—
heavy-hearted,
weeping,
gnashing my teeth.[4]

In Your mercy,
You sought me out,[5]

1. Heb. 13:15. 2. 1 Cor. 7:31. 3. Ps. 16:11. 4. Luke 13:28. 5. Luke 19:10.

cradled me in Your arms,
brought me home.[6]

Now,
bound to Your Spirit,[7]
my strength is renewed[8]—
in test and trial
I am refined;[9]
sanctified in suffering.[10]

You speak to me
in the secret place:[11]
"Come away from lifeless loves,
from all that leaves you
hollow
and hungry.
Take My yoke upon you
and learn from Me,
for I am gentle
and lowly in heart,
and you will find rest for your soul."[12]

Fill me with Your Spirit, Lord.
Slake my thirst with the water of life[13]—
for I am made for covenant love,[14]
and my soul is restless
until it finds its rest in You.[15]

On my best days,
I am half-deaf,
half-dead:
peering through a glass, darkly.[16]

6. Matt. 18:12–14. 7. Song of Sol. 2:16. 8. Ps. 84:7. 9. 1 Pet. 1:7.
10. James 1:4. 11. Ps. 91:1. 12. Matt. 11:28–30. 13. John 4:10. 14. Deut. 6:5.
15. Inspired by Augustine, *Confessions* 1.1.1. 16. 1 Cor. 13:12.

I hear Your voice,
perceive Your presence,
and still I turn away.

Why do I resist Your embrace?
Run from Your grace?

I languish in
body,
mind,
spirit,
while You battle evil on my behalf—
routing darkness,
covering me with Your kindness,
sheltering me,
a sinner,
under the shadow of mercy.[17]

In Your patience,
You whisper:
"Hear.
Heed.
Follow.
Feast."

In You, Lord,
are all the desires of my heart:[18]
my longings,
yearnings,
hopes,
expectations.

In You
and You alone,
my soul finds rest.[19]

Amen.

17. Ps. 57:1. 18. Ps. 37:4. 19. Ps. 62:1.

PSALM 82

JUSTICE AT LAST

Lord God,
the good world You made
has been ravaged by sin,
ransacked by wickedness—
a temple desecrated,
a garden choked by weeds.

Meanwhile,
You reign over the chaos of human conquest:
King of kings,
God of gods.

How long will evil win?
How long will darkness spread its
veil of violence over the earth?

In time,
justice will be done;
mercy will be the law of the land—
the poor exalted,
the captives freed.[1]
No more harm will befall
those who have no strength,
no defense,
no voice.

But as we wait,
the rulers of earth wreak havoc.
Deaf to Your voice,
blind to Your face,

1. Luke 4:18–19.

they suppress the truth[2]—
spiraling into darkness,
dragging creation down with them.

If only they could know the high calling of humanity:
to be priests in the kingdom of God:[3]
Guardians of Grace.
Cultivators.
Creators.
Colaborers.[4]
Covenant-Keepers.

In their greed,
they have forfeited their calling.
Squandered their inheritance.

Lord,
May Your justice roll like the waves of the sea,
Your righteousness like a river[5]—
bright as crystal,
leading to Your throne.[6]

For from You
and through You
and for You
are all things[7]—
thrones,
dominions,
powers.[8]
You reign over all.
Beside You
there is no other.[9]

Amen.

2. Rom. 1:18–19. 3. Exod. 19:5–6; 1 Pet. 2:9. 4. 1 Cor. 3:9. 5. Amos 5:24. 6. Rev. 22:1. 7. Rom. 11:36. 8. Col. 1:16. 9. Isa. 45:5.

PSALM 83

THE GOOD FIGHT

Spirit of God,
who is my enemy?

My dust-born brother?
Spirit-born sister?

What field of battle awaits me?[1]
What weapons of war?
What bloodshed?
What sorrow?

Is the enemy of my soul
not all that stands against You—
evil in all its guises,
shameless in its conquest;
a marauding,
desecrating
darkness?

My fight is not against flesh and blood,
but against principalities,
powers,
forces of evil.[2]

What foe awaits me?
What adversary plots my destruction?

Forgive me when I make
my enemies
Your enemies;
when I turn my prayers toward

1. 1 Tim. 6:12. 2. Eph. 6:12.

the defeat of those
named only by me.

Your foes
are more fierce,
more insidious,
than any human face
set against me.

May I stand fast
against all that stands
against You.

May I turn inward
to face the darkness at work within—
that I may be wholehearted,[3]
free from the bondage of sin.[4]

Who is my enemy, Lord?
Who would snuff me out?
Rob the life
from my spirit?

Does evil not go by many names?
Accusation.[5]
Hatred.
Despair.
Chaos.
Arrogance.
Unfaithfulness.
Fear.
Pride.

Fill me with Your Spirit,
that I may have the strength to withstand,
to vanquish terror and temptation—

3. Ps. 86:11. 4. Gal. 5:1. 5. Rev. 12:10.

to partner with You
in the undoing of the works of darkness.[6]

May I be called
Blessing.
Joy Giver.
Shalom Bearer.
Faithful Friend.
Cruciform Soul.

To be like You, Lord Jesus,[7]
is my deepest desire:
to abide in You,[8]
walk with You—
Your truth about my waist,
Your righteousness about my heart,
feet propelled by the ready proclamation of Your Gospel,
head covered in the helmet of Your salvation,
sword of the Spirit in one hand,
shield of faith in the other.[9]

In Your strength,
may I scatter darkness,
conquer wickedness.

Let all that stands against You
be utterly consumed:
a forest razed by fire,
a hovel flattened by wind.

May all who resist You
crawl to the foot of Your cross
and there lay down their arms.

In Your mercy,
may they be enemies no more.[10]

6. 1 John 3:8. 7. Eph. 5:1–2. 8. John 15:4–5. 9. Eph. 6:13–17. 10. Matt. 5:44.

PSALM 84

RESTLESS

Lord,
Your heart is the home I long for—
haven in storm,
refuge in chaos—
door unlatched,
table prepared for me.[1]

How I long for that place:
to cease from my labors,
to dwell beneath the shelter of Your presence.[2]

I am restless for You.

You are a canopy of trees,
branches flecked with birds—
a motley menagerie.

You are a banquet hall,
table laden with food and drink—
a joyful revelry.

You are creation's resting place—
a garden uncontainable,
unstoppable;
an unending wellspring of life.[3]

Hear the song of Your people, Lord:
blessing
and honor
and praise
for Your infinite kindness![4]

1. Ps. 23:5. 2. Ps. 91:1. 3. John 4:14. 4. Eph. 2:7.

In my weakness,
be my strength.[5]
In my wandering,
be my bearing.
Then goodness and mercy will chase me;[6]
life will pursue me.
In the land of dead and dying things,
I will flourish—
a desert flower sustained by Your grace.

Help me to know You are near, Lord—
that You hear me,
see me,
delight in me—
for I have no abiding home here,
no enduring rest in these shadowed lands.

But You have prepared a place for me[7]—
greater than the halls of kings,
the comforts of the strong—
a place where I will dwell with You forever.[8]

You are light of my eyes
and strength of my life—
the Giver of All Good Things.
You shower me with blessings,
with every good and perfect gift.[9]

What an honor it is
to live in Your house,
to feast at Your table,
to rest in Your presence.[10]

Amen.

5. 2 Cor. 12:10. 6. Ps. 23:6. 7. John 14:2. 8. Ps. 23:6. 9. James 1:17.
10. Matt. 11:28.

PSALM 85

THE FACE OF GOD IN CHRIST

Love has a name,
a countenance,
a heart
that bears our sorrows,[1]
shoulders our grief,
exposes our weakness,
atones for our sins[2]*—*
revealing,
in radiant glory,[3]
the face of God in Christ.[4]

Look upon me, Lord,
with renewing,
refreshing life.
See beyond my brokenness,
my ceaseless struggle—
my trespasses,
transgressions;
all I have done
and left undone.[5]

May my daughters thrive,
my sons flourish,
the children
of my children
walk in the light of mercy.[6]

1. Isa. 53:4. 2. 1 John 2:2. 3. Heb. 1:3. 4. 2 Cor. 4:6. 5. Episcopal Church, *The Book of Common Prayer and Administration of the Sacraments and Other Rites and Ceremonies of the Church* (New York: Oxford University Press, 1990), 360. 6. Luke 1:78–79.

Deliver me,
I pray,
from the casual embrace of death;
from the despair
of my desire.

Reclaim me.
Restore me—
that I may hear Your voice,
walk in Your ways,
to the glory of Your name—
for You have made Yourself known to me;[7]
called me Your beloved.[8]

In You,
all that is
good,
beautiful,
true,
holy,
worthy,
joyous—
converges and embraces.[9]

Everywhere I look,
I see the loving hand of God:
the earth gives seed,
the heavens, rain:
abundant kindness,
endless mercy—
the harvest of Your righteous rule.

Love has a name,
a countenance,
a heart

7. John 17:26. 8. Jer. 31:3. 9. Phil. 4:8.

that bears our sorrows,
shoulders our grief,
exposes our weakness,
atones for our sins—
revealing,
in radiant glory,
the face of God in Christ.

PSALM 86

IN TIME

Lord God,
I am desperate for You—
for Your nearness,
Your touch,
Your voice.

Where else can I go,
when You are the only refuge?[1]

All my hope is in You.
All my desire is for You.[2]
In the din of voices,
hear my cry, Lord.

Do not let me fall by the wayside—
cast off,
pitied,
forgotten.

Have mercy on me, Son of David.[3]

At Your touch,
will my mourning not become dancing?[4]
My weeping become singing?[5]
Are You not King of the Feast?
The Joyful Lord of New Creation,
who welcomes all who come
from north and south,
east and west,
to recline at Your table?[6]

1. Ps. 46:1. 2. Song of Sol. 7:10. 3. Matt. 20:30. 4. Ps. 30:11. 5. Ps. 30:5. 6. Luke 13:29.

Though I have wandered from Your ways
and suffered the shame of separation,
You have clothed me in Your goodness,
seated me in a place of honor[7]—
called me a child of God.

Hear me in my desperation,
in my heartsick longing.
Your name is a word in my mouth,
in my heart—
tumbled syllables on the tongue;
a rock worn smooth in water.

In the depths of my despair,
You will not abandon me.
In Your time,
You will answer.

What god is known for kindness?
What deity, carved in clay,
sculpted in stone,
is praised for faithfulness?
Worshiped for goodness?
You alone are God,
and there is none beside You.[8]

In time,
all will know You,
from the least
to the greatest,
and praise You
as You rightly deserve.

As for me,
I will not wait for Kingdom Come
to sing Your song.

7. Luke 14:10. 8. Deut. 32:39.

I will walk Your path
in the here
and the now—
when the ground is uneven
and storm clouds gather.

By the power of Your Spirit, I will be
Full-hearted.[9]
Single-minded.
Thankful.
Soulful.
Willful.

For You have shouldered the burden of my sin.
Lifted me from the grave.
Crowned me with life.[10]

Yet I am hated on account of You:
scorned for my devotion,
mocked for my faithfulness.

In a lost world,
I tread on enemy soil.

But in Your eyes,
I am favored.[11]
Accepted.[12]
Cherished.[13]

In Your mercy,
You have turned a face of kindness upon me.
Everywhere I go,
I am followed by Your faithfulness.[14]

What reason have I to doubt You now?
You will deliver me from this darkness.

9. Ps. 86:11. 10. Ps. 103:4. 11. Ps. 84:11. 12. John 6:37. 13. 1 John 4:11. 14. Ps. 23:6.

My strength will be renewed.
In due time,
with fresh vigor,
I will spread my wings
and soar above this chaos—
for I have waited patiently for You.[15]

May all who oppose me
see Your gracious hand upon me,
Your mercy surrounding me,
Your love renewing me—
and may they rue the day
they turned from You.

15. Isa. 40:31.

PSALM 87

CITY OF GOD

Beyond the veil of time,
above the march of history
and the affairs of humankind
stands the City of God:
cosmic citadel of New Creation,
jewel of the patient Kingdom of Christ,
Eternal Home of His Covenant Bride.[1]

Word,
breath,
song—
uttered across
ages,
centuries,
millennia—
tells the story of the Most High King
who dwells among us,[2]
who calls us sons and daughters[3]—
seating us in places of honor,
showering us with blessing.

Through the power of Your Spirit,
may we give as we have been given to,
bless as we have been blessed—
that we might advance Your kingdom in the earth:
seeking the lost,
guiding them home.

Sing!
For the dwelling place of God is with us.

1. Rev. 19:7. 2. John 1:14. 3. 2 Cor. 6:18.

We are His people;
He is our King[4]—
from His fullness
we have all received
grace
upon
grace
upon
grace.[5]

4. Rev. 21:3. 5. John 1:16.

PSALM 88

HOPE BEYOND THE GRAVE

Christ,
my only hope in life and death,
fan the flames of trust within me.

I twist and groan in the dark,
pining for deliverance,
aching for comfort—
the steady voice of Your Spirit,
to tell me this is not the end.

If You have ever heard me, Lord,
hear me now.

I am saddled with sorrows:
a wraith haunting the land of the living.

Death beckons,
inviting me to cease from my labors,
to give up the ghost,
to slip into the quiet surrender of the grave,
buried so deep
that I would be utterly forgotten.

In Your sovereignty,
is it not Your hand that has dealt this blow?
Your judgment that has fallen upon me?
Your anger that foams like an angry sea about me,
thrashing me against the rocks?

Is it not Your will
that my friends have abandoned me?

That I am cut off from the living—
a phantom of my former self,
wasting away in the darkness?

I groan for deliverance.
My faith wears thin.

Tell me,
is there hope beyond the grave?
Can Your mercy reach me there,
if I pass from the land of the living?

Did You not descend into hell,[1]
into utter darkness,
to claim the keys of death?[2]
In You,
will the dead not be raised
to life imperishable?[3]

How long will I suffer this silence?
How long will Your face be turned from me?
How long will pain be my constant companion,[4]
crippling fear my closest friend?
How long must I live beneath the shadow of wrath?
Crushed beneath the weight of affliction?
Abandoned?
Besieged?
Betrayed?

I have no one to turn to
but You, Lord.

And so I wait.[5]

1. Eph. 4:7–10; inspired by the Apostles' Creed. 2. Rev. 1:18.
3. 1 Cor. 15:42. 4. Ps. 38:17. 5. Ps. 37:7.

PSALM 89

THE LOVE OF CHRIST

Father,
may my life be an unending song:
ceaseless praise
for Your infinite kindness:
holy hymnody,
echoing for generations to come.[1]

How can I voice all You have done?
The grace You have given?[2]
The face of mercy turned to me?

The love of Christ endures forever.[3]

Like all the saints before me,
my life is a story of
promises made,
covenants kept—
the favor of God
made manifest
in space and time.

The love of Christ endures forever.

I join with all the hosts of heaven:
seen,
unseen,
celestial choirs,
elders,
archangels,
ministering spirits,

1. Ps. 45:17. 2. Eph. 4:7. 3. Rom. 8:37–39; Ps. 138:8.

singing the glory of the One
who was
and is
and is to come.[4]

I have searched the earth,
peered into holy mysteries,
listened to the chanting of the wise,
sat at the feet of holy ones—
but there is nothing to compare with You, Lord:
the God of Faithful Love.
You are worthy of all praise.[5]

The love of Christ endures forever.

You are Lord of the Sea,
King of surging waves
and placid streams.

You rule and reign
over chaos,
darkness,
death.

There is no land that is not Yours—
no territory,
principality,
distant plot
of earth's domain
that does not bear Your mark.

Mountains sing "Holy,"
fields shout "Hallelujah"—
the work of Your hands praises You
for Your kindness,[6]

4. Rev. 4:8. 5. Ps. 145:3. 6. Eph. 2:4–7.

Your might,
Your truth.[7]

You alone sit on the throne of creation.[8]

The beloved of God
join Your endless feast:
the festival of the faithful—
singing glory,
honor,
praise,[9]
to Him who loves us,
atones for us,
intercedes for us,[10]
delights in us.[11]

As I tread this well-worn path,
may I be anointed with the oil of Your gladness,[12]
emboldened by the strength of Your presence—
Speaking the Word of God.
Walking in the Way of God.
Led by the Vision of God.

Give me the strength
to slay giants,[13]
the wisdom
to outwit wickedness,
the strength to stand
when others fall—
for the battle is Yours.[14]

Every victory
is a mercy,
every triumph
a sign
of Your relentless faithfulness to me.

7. John 8:31–32. 8. Ps. 99:1–3. 9. Ps. 66:1–2. 10. Rom. 8:34–35. 11. Zeph. 3:17. 12. Isa. 61:3. 13. 1 Sam. 17:1–58. 14. 1 Sam. 17:47.

The love of Christ endures forever.

You are a stone in the river,
a steady place to stand
in the midst of rushing waters.

I am Your beloved:
child of Your covenant—
seated at Your table,
arrayed in Your righteousness,[15]
one with You forever.

How often have I failed
to follow Your way?[16]
To heed Your
Word,
wisdom,
counsel?

I deserve discipline,
distance,
darkness—
but You have compassion for me;
Your kindness leads me to repentance.[17]

Though I am not worthy,
You have chosen me,
delighted in me,
called me an heir of the King.

What can break Your covenant?
Violate Your vow?

As long as the day and the night
come at their appointed time,
Your Word stands.[18]

15. Isa. 61:10. 16. Ps. 25:4. 17. Rom. 2:4. 18. Ps. 119:89.

But now,
where have You gone, Lord?
In desperate need,
inner torment,
it is as if You have turned from me;[19]
my life is in ruins.

Are You not the One who passed through the flame?
Who pledged Your own sacrifice?[20]

I am dust-drawn,
name-cursed—
a hollowed-out shell,
an object of ridicule.

No victory.
No flourishing.
No pride.
No peace.

Is my glory—
gifted,
given
by You,
reflection of Your image,[21]
refraction of Your light—
now my shame?

Will I be known as
"once loved"?
"Once delivered"?
"Once cherished"?

Fear grips me.

Am I nothing more than dust?
Does the Spirit of God not live within me?[22]

19. Ps. 88:14. 20. Heb. 9:13–14. 21. Phil. 2:15. 22. Rom. 8:11.

Time wears thin.
Patience withers.
All I know is suffering and grief.

Come to me again, Lord.
Fill me with Your peace.

Humanity is vain,
vaporous,
volatile—
seeking momentary pleasures,
fleeting fame—
while the shadow of death
looms over us all.

Remember me, Lord,
in the night of my anguish,
the season of my suffering.

I cling to Your promises:[23]
that the enemies of my soul
will yield to Your power,
that the darkness that afflicts me
is destined for destruction—
for Your Word will not return in vain.[24]

Even in my weakness,
I will praise You.[25]
Broken as I am,
Your name will be on my lips.[26]

The love of Christ endures forever.

23. 2 Cor. 1:20. 24. Isa. 55:11. 25. Ps. 42:11. 26. Ps. 63:3–4.

PSALM 90

A NEW BEGINNING

Father,
for as long as humankind has roamed the earth,
wandering east of Eden,[1]
we have longed for the comfort of Your house,
the shelter of Your arms.[2]

Beyond the boundaries of space,
time,
matter,
there is only You:
Creator.
Sustainer.
Storyteller.

We live
and we die:
A fleeting breath.
A passing mention.
A drop in the ocean of eternity.

No sooner has the light filled our eyes
than it dims,
and darkness envelops us.

We are driftwood,
carried to shore on the tide,
then washed away again.

We are flora,
vibrant and flourishing,

1. Gen. 4:16. 2. Nah. 1:7.

before our color withers
and we descend to the deep from which we came.

How many of us,
brought to life by Your breath,
choose to haunt the paths of the dead?
Rejecting Your truth,
we court destruction,
welcome judgment,
become what we worship—
chasing passing pleasure
over abiding satisfaction,
ephemeral delight
over eternal joy.

We wander in desert wastes,
youth and vitality
slipping from our grasp
like water through a sieve,
until we give up the ghost.

Such is the fate of all who scorn You,
who walk according to their own wisdom,
who insist upon their own way.

Teach me to walk in humility before You,[3]
conscious of my weakness,[4]
my finiteness,
my limitations,
that I may make the most
of the time I have been given.

Restore to me the years the locusts have eaten.[5]
May all that is dead in me
be resurrected,

3. Mic. 6:8. 4. 2 Cor. 12:10. 5. Joel 2:25.

that I may walk with renewed purpose
and replenished joy—
a testimony to Your redeeming work.

For You do not hold my wasted time against me,
the hours and days and years I have squandered.
With gentleness,
You grant me a new beginning.[6]

May Your mercy be manifest in me,
and in my children,
and my children's children.

In all that I set my heart and mind to do,
grant Your blessing,
that my life would bear abundant fruit[7]
for Your kingdom.

Amen.

6. 2 Cor. 5:17. 7. Gal. 5:22–23.

PSALM 91

ABIDE IN CHRIST

Abide,
O my soul;
abide in Christ alone.[1]

Remain
in intimate union,[2]
enduring peace,[3]
abundant joy,
continual delight.

No wandering
the wide earth
seeking sanctuary,
solace,
salvation
in interim inns.

Abide,
O my soul;
abide in Christ alone.

Where have I to go, Lord,
but the shelter of Your arms?
The shadow of Your mercy?

You are the One Safe Place:
my comfort and confidence,
my strength and song.[4]

You break the ties that bind me,
heal the sickness that afflicts me.

1. John 15:4. 2. Gal. 2:20. 3. John 14:27. 4. Exod. 15:12.

I am cradled in the wings of grace:
beloved of God,
safe in Your keeping;
if You are for me,
who can be against me?[5]

When evil pursues me,
when affliction and devastation plague me,
I will not give in to fear or flight;[6]
I will press in,
deeper still,
shielded by Your faithfulness.

Abide,
O my soul;
abide in Christ alone.

The battle rages around me:
death and destruction,
sorrow and suffering—
but I am safe in the arms of God.
I will watch as darkness falls,
as death is swallowed up in victory.[7]

For the world is passing away,
along with its desires—
but all who walk in Your will
abide forever.[8]

I am kept
by mercies
known
and unknown—
by the wind of the Spirit,
ministering angels,
a hedge of protection around me.[9]

5. Rom. 8:31. 6. Rom. 8:15. 7. 1 Cor. 15:54–55. 8. 1 John 2:17. 9. Job 1:10.

From what death have You saved me?
From what pain have You spared me?
My life is in Your hands.

Abide,
O my soul;
abide in Christ alone.

You are
Father,
Defender,
Savior,
Lifter of My Head[10]—
and I am Your beloved,
child of the Most High God.[11]

Never have You forsaken
those who seek You.[12]

In the quiet of the night,
You speak life to me.
In times of trouble,
You preserve me.[13]

I endure
by Your countless mercies,
Your unmerited grace.

Abide,
O my soul;
abide in Christ alone.

10. Ps. 3:3. 11. Ps. 131:2. 12. Ps. 9:10. 13. Ps. 119:50.

PSALM 92

SONG OF MY LIFE

Lord,
it is a gift to wake to this Sabbath day—
eyes open to look upon Your grace,
etched in tree and cloud,
echoed by wind and bird.
Everywhere I turn,
I am greeted by Your kindness.

Gratitude wells up in me—
steadying lightness,
sustaining song,
the anthem of these waking hours.

When night draws its shade across the sky,
I rest in peace,
surrounded by Your mercy.

This is the truth of my life:
though undeserving,
I am loved by the King[1]
of heaven and earth—
invited to His table,
ushered into His rest.

The wise among us
study,
scrutinize,
ponder,
pontificate—
but merely scratch the surface
of Your created world.

1. 1 John 3:2.

They seize knowledge,
only to be met with further mystery:
a universe expanding,
galaxy upon galaxy—
the fathomless canvas of God.

Yet they have the arrogance
to ignore You,
deny You,
reject You.

For a time,
they conquer,
colonize,
captivate,
subjugate—
forgetting that understanding
is found at Your feet;[2]
that all treasures of wisdom and knowledge
are hidden in Your heart;[3]
that all who shun You,
who mock Your grace,
pity Your passion,
will suffer the terrible silence of God,
cleaved from the living
by an impassable void.

But You delight in me,
filling me with new strength,
anointing me with the joy of Your presence.[4]

I will watch as darkness is defeated;
as every enemy of my soul is
disarmed,
demobilized,
devoted to destruction.

2. Prov. 9:10. 3. Col. 2:3. 4. Ps. 45:7.

The beloved of God
are a forest of trees—
oak,
cedar,
redwood,
palm—
fertile and flourishing
in the grove of Your planting.

We go from strength to strength:[5]
life everlasting,
light unending,
brighter
and brighter
until full day,[6]
when we enter Your eternal rest[7]
and labor no more.

5. Ps. 84:7. 6. Prov. 4:18. 7. Matt. 11:28.

PSALM 93

EVERLASTING GOD

Lord,
one truth stands above all others:
You are King,[1]
and there is none beside You.[2]

For who can speak
worlds into being?
Who can breathe life
into dust?[3]

Ancient stones
proclaim it.
Timeless words
declare it.
You are Everlasting God:
Alpha.
Omega.
Beginning.
End.[4]

Your Word-shaped world
gives You praise:
glory surging from the deep,
the roar of wave
upon wave—
thunderous worship,
exalting Your name.

Lord,
one truth stands above all others:

1. Ps. 95:3. 2. Isa. 45:5. 3. Gen. 2:7. 4. Rev. 22:13.

You are King,
and there is none beside You.

Your Word stands,[5]
generation to generation;
not one iota,
not one dot,
will pass from it
until all is fulfilled.

5. 1 Pet. 1:22–25.

PSALM 94

A BLIGHT UPON THE EARTH

Father God,
there is a blight upon the earth,
a wasting sickness
in the hearts of the wicked.

Their depravity is boundless,
their hubris, heartless,
their insolence, endless.
Truly there is nothing new under the sun—
still, they plot and scheme,
seeking new methods to their madness.

Without hesitation,
they trample the innocent;
the vulnerable are gathered like chaff for the fire
as the wicked turn a blind eye to the suffering
they have sown—
godless,
graceless,
they pay You no mind.

But the hands that do violence
were made by You.
The feet that trample the innocent
were made by You.
The mouths that spew curses
were made by You.

For what are we
apart from You?

What breath have we
but Yours?
What strength have we
but that which You have given us?

You are,
therefore we are.

We are by no means
autonomous,
self-sufficient,
self-sustaining.

You must draw us to Yourself;
guide us in the Way of Life.[1]

The fear of the Lord
is the beginning of wisdom;
only fools despise Your instruction.[2]

You are the eternal Sabbath,
inviting us to rest from our labors,
to take Your yoke upon us.

My burdens are many,
but Your burden is light.[3]

Though I am often
faithless,
fickle,
fallen,
Your promises stand.
What You began in me
will be finished.[4]
This story will reach its fitting end.

1. Ps. 16:11. 2. Prov. 1:7. 3. Matt. 11:28–30. 4. Phil. 1:6.

For all the wayward people of God:
all sinful saints,
all pride-plagued lovers of Christ—
our suffering will not be in vain.

We will be one with You,
whole and healed at last,
when You rid this earth of wickedness,
and death is no more.[5]

Where would I be
without Your saving grace?
What pit of darkness
would I call home
without Your guiding hand?

Like all broken images of God,
I am drawn deathward,
pulled by sin's gravity.

But in Your mercy,
You have saved me
from the lust of my heart
and the stain of the world.

How?
In what indiscernible way
have You held me?
What wind-like pattern of grace
has sustained me?

Somehow,
in the night,
a song.[6]

5. 1 Cor. 15:54. 6. Ps. 77:6.

Only that which dies
and lives again
can be Yours.

May I be one with You, Lord—
united in Your death
and resurrection,[7]
a New Creation
groaning for New Creation.[8]

The prideful,
the hell-bent,
the willfully godless,
flourish for a time—
but You will rise
to judge the living and the dead,
and who can stand before You?[9]

7. Rom. 6:5. 8. Rom. 8:26. 9. Ps. 76:7.

PSALM 95

WELLSPRING OF WORSHIP

Lord God,
as I sing Your praise,
You renew me,
restore me,
rebuild me.

I am a grateful child of the King,[1]
filled with the harmonies of New Creation—
seeking to honor You,
bless You,
exalt You—
for You are
great,
glorious,
magnificent,
merciful.

What words can I bring
to voice what is
ineffable,
unfathomable,
inconceivable?

You are the
immortal,
immovable,
illimitable,
immeasurable
God:

1. Gal. 4:6–7.

Lord of all things,
for whom all things exist,
to whom all things bow.[2]

Deepest depth
to highest height,
fathomless abyss
to lofty star;
field,
plain,
canyon,
sea,
is fashioned by Your hand,[3]
upheld by Your hand.

My heart is a wellspring of worship,
spilling
adoration,
exaltation,
veneration
as I bow before You,
the One True God.[4]

Shepherd me, Lord.
Guide me to places of rest:
further up,
further in.[5]

Give me a hearing heart, Lord,
a listening spirit.
Do not let me grow
cold,
deaf,

2. Phil. 2:9–11. 3. Ps. 104:24. 4. Deut. 6:4. 5. "Further up, further in" is a phrase borrowed from C. S. Lewis, *The Last Battle* (1956, 1984; repr., New York: HarperCollins, 2000), 205.

stiff-necked,[6]
strong-willed.

By Your grace,
keep me from aimlessness,
faithlessness,
endless wandering.

In Your mercy,
may I enter Your rest.[7]
Amen.

6. Acts 7:51. 7. Heb. 4:9–10.

PSALM 96

BEAUTY AND GRANDEUR

Father God,
be praised by all You have made!
May all that lives and breathes
live and breathe for Your glory![1]
May the earth resound with singing;
the Gospel of Your grace
a joyful melody
echoing throughout all creation.

May the Story be told
again and again
until every heart has heard,
every soul has been fed.[2]

Many worship what they do not know,
while salvation is in You:[3]
desire of nations,[4]
longing of every human heart.[5]

All beauty and grandeur is Yours:
the might of mountains,
the dew of the morning—
all that moves the heart
and stirs the soul
is Your handiwork
and Your glory.[6]

Oh, that everyone would worship You!

1. Ps. 150:6. 2. Matt. 28:18–20. 3. John 4:22. 4. Hag. 2:7. 5. Resonates with a line in the hymn "Come, Thou Long Expected Jesus" (1744) by Charles Wesley. 6. Ps. 19:1.

Every man,
woman,
child,
filled with awe
at the work of Your hands
and the miracle of Your mercy!

If all could see with clear eyes
and unhindered hearts,[7]
would they not fall before You,
holding nothing back,
sacrificing all?[8]

May I proclaim Your Lordship
to those with ears to hear.
May I sing of Your eternal power,
divine nature,
righteous wrath,
fathomless grace.

Creation groans,[9]
longing to shake free from its bondage:
Stars, planets, galaxies sing:
"Soon!"[10]

Mountains, oceans, vineyards reply:
"Very soon!"

Mighty oaks, towering cedars, creak, sway, say:
"How long?"

How long, Lord,
until You rise in judgment
to cleanse this world of wickedness;
to welcome Your children
into Your eternal rest?[11]

7. 1 Cor. 13:12. 8. Rom. 12:1–2. 9. Rom. 8:22. 10. Rev. 22:12. 11. Heb. 4:9–10.

PSALM 97

THE LORD RULES AND REIGNS

The sky is a banner unfurled, proclaiming,
"The Lord reigns!"
Inlet, shore, peak, plain declare:
"The Lord rules over all!"[1]

You are shrouded in mystery,
clothed in majesty:
radiant King of Glory,
dissolving
dross and darkness.

The sky groans,
clouds pierced with streaks of light,
flickering over the wide earth.
Creation bows in wonder before You.

You have made Yourself known to all—
Your eternal power,
divine nature,
evident in all You have made.[2]

Those who turn from Your glory
to the worship of lesser things
become fools—
their thinking futile,
their foolish hearts darkened.[3]

May every false god bow,
every idol be broken before You!

1. Ps. 103:19. 2. Rom. 1:20. 3. Rom. 1:21–23.

The people of God
delight in Your ways—
feasting on Your kindness,
proclaiming the glories of the One
who loved us,
gave Himself for us,
raised us to new life.

Lord,
in Your mercy,
give me a hunger for righteousness,
a hatred of wickedness—
that I may abhor evil,
hold fast to what is good.[4]

Abiding in You,[5]
You in me,
I rest secure—
growing in grace,
Your face shining upon me,[6]
Your joy my strength.[7]

The sky is a banner unfurled, proclaiming,
"The Lord reigns!"

Truly You are Lord over all!

4. Rom. 12:9. 5. John 15:4–5. 6. Num. 6:25. 7. Neh. 8:10.

PSALM 98

NEW SONGS

Father God,
though You are
ancient,
ageless,
unbound by time[1]—
You have worked Your will in human history,
Your salvation in space-time—
and we,
Your children,
are still finding new songs to sing,
new praises to bring,
new grammar to proclaim[2]
the length,
height,
depth,
breadth
of Your kindness to us.

With power
You have disarmed darkness,
trampled evil,
raised us to new life with Christ.[3]

Your Gospel of grace
has run to the ends of the earth,
proclaiming freedom to the captives,
peace to the downcast,[4]
life to the dead.

1. Ps. 90:2. 2. Ps. 40:3. 3. Rom. 6:4. 4. Isa. 61:1–3; Luke 4:18–19.

For all with eyes to see
and ears to hear,
the truth has been made manifest.

You have not abandoned us[5]
nor forsaken us.
You have been true to Your Word:
Faithful.
Steadfast.
Unwavering.
Unchanging.

In time,
the earth will be filled with Your glory—
a cup overflowing,[6]
joy upon joy,
everlasting!

Hear the song of the redeemed—
this merry cavalcade,
spilling into street and byway,
every instrument tuned to give You praise.

May all creation sing along:
wind
and wave,
sun
and stars,
singing
"Holy!"

For You are good,
and in You there is no darkness,
nor shadow due to change.[7]

5. Ps. 16:10. 6. Ps. 23:5. 7. James 1:17.

Come, Lord!
Judge the earth,
that evil might be vanquished,
and Your kingdom reign forever.[8]
Amen.

8. Luke 1:31–33.

PSALM 99

HOLY, HOLY, HOLY

Perfect in love,
in unity,[1]
the Lord our God—
holy, holy, holy.[2]

Luminous presence,
blessed incarnation,[3]
the Lord our God—
holy, holy, holy.

Centrifugal goodness,
centripetal grace,
the Lord our God—
holy, holy, holy.

My soul exalts You:[4]
great,
awesome,
just,
kind,
the Lord our God—
holy, holy, holy.

I worship in the place
where Your glory dwells,[5]
a priest in the kingdom of God:[6]
keeper of the Way,
mediator of glory—
adorned in righteousness,
ushered beyond the veil.

1. Inspired by the hymn "Holy, Holy, Holy, Lord God Almighty" (1826) by Reginald Heber. 2. Isa. 6:3; Rev. 4:8. 3. John 1:14. 4. Ps. 145:1–2. 5. Ps. 26:8. 6. 1 Pet. 2:9.

In Your mercy, You
Answer.
Forgive.
Avenge.
Restore.

My soul exalts You:
great,
awesome,
just,
kind,
the Lord our God—
holy, holy, holy.

PSALM 100

HOLY GROUND

Father God,
may all the work of Your hands praise You today.[1]
May all God-breathed things—
all beauteous,
glorious,
savage
things—
sing the glories of Your grace!

May we—
image bearers,[2]
stewards of creation,
the rescued and redeemed—
know the face of our Father,[3]
rest in the shelter of Your presence.

Every tree is a pillar,
every stone an altar,
in the temple of creation.

May we tread carefully—
with gratitude,
worship,
and wonder—
for we walk on holy ground,[4]
debtors to Your kindness,
mercy,
and love.
You are with us always,
even to the end of the age.[5]
Amen.

1. Ps. 92:4. 2. Gen. 1:27. 3. Ps. 27:8. 4. Acts 7:33. 5. Matt. 28:20.

PSALM 101

I WAIT FOR YOU

Father,
I return to the fundamentals
of the faith:
Your endless love,
merciful justice—
the path of the righteous,
the way of freedom.[1]

Meet me, I pray,
in this humble home;
I wait for You.

May I resist the pull
of lesser loves,
the downward gravity of the Fall.

I have seen too many dying things:
withered,
lifeless,
colorless.

Keep me on Your path, Lord:
heart pure,[2]
vision clear[3]—
lest I become the very thing I despise:
one who was enlightened,
who walked in the way of the Spirit,
tasted the goodness of God,
then fell away.[4]

May I forsake evil
in pursuit of a

1. Gal. 5:1. 2. Matt. 5:8. 3. 1 Cor. 13:12. 4. Heb. 6:4–6.

wholehearted
hunger for holiness.

Help me, Lord.
I am surrounded by careless tongues:
those who curse,
accuse,
damn,
defame—
who take when they should give,[5]
tear down when they should build.
By their words they will be condemned.[6]

But I will gather about me
the godly,
the gracious,
the meek,
the merciful:
all who love Your way—
for in an abundance of counselors
there is safety.[7]

Those who lie,
cheat,
steal,
will have no place at my table.

Day by day,
at the rising of the sun,
I will arm myself with Your Spirit,
strengthen myself with Your Word.[8]

For darkness threatens to swallow
all that is good
and holy
and true—
but I refuse to go down without a fight.[9]

5. Acts 20:35. 6. Matt. 12:37. 7. Prov. 15:22. 8. Phil. 4:13. 9. 1 Tim. 6:12.

PSALM 102

WIND-SCATTERED

Lord,
when I am burdened with sorrow,
may Your face shine upon me.[1]
When I suffer in silence,
may Your words speak life to me.

Christ, be near.[2]

What would I liken this suffering to?

I am a slow-burning tree—
flames rising from the roots:
branch-withered,
leaf-shriveled,
strength-sapped,
wind-scattered.

I am a nocturnal shadow,
eternally restless,
stalking the moonlit world,
haunting sleeping towns.

I am a vulgar word
in the mouth of the damned;
skin and bones
hugging the pavement,
facedown in filth.

I am debris,
swept into the gutter,
carried away on the breeze.

1. Ps. 31:16. 2. James 4:8.

Christ,
have You cursed me?
Am I cut off from You?
Has Your Spirit departed from me?[3]

Are You not Lord of all?
Will Your grace not reach me,
even here?

Your people wander—
but there are some of us still
who cling to the hope of the Risen One;
who search for signs of life
amid the wreckage of the world.

There will be a day
when sorrow subsides,
when the sun rises with healing in its wings,[4]
when all the earth stands in awestruck wonder
at Your power
and majesty
and dominion.

You will build up the ancient ruins,
repair former devastations,[5]
establish Your eternal city—
the sunless,
moonless
Citadel of New Creation,
radiant with Your glory.[6]

You are not deaf to our groaning,
aloof to our pain.
You are with us in our suffering,
until the end of the age.[7]

3. Ps. 51:11. 4. Mal. 4:2. 5. Isa. 61:4. 6. Rev. 21:23. 7. Matt. 28:20.

May the Story be told,
in ink,
blood,
breath,
silence,
song,
feast,
famine,
pain,
joy:
that God,
in His great mercy,
descended into our darkness,
took on human flesh,
walked among us,[8]
proclaimed the coming kingdom;
suffered,
bled and died,
shook free from death—
to save us from sin,
from the power of Satan,
from the sway of lesser loves.

Be praised, Lord!
The stone that the builders rejected
has become the cornerstone.
It is marvelous in our eyes![9]

As I bear this mantle of affliction,
will You give me strength
to carry on a little while longer?
To limp,
stagger,
perhaps even,

8. John 1:14. 9. Ps. 118:22–23.

by Your grace,
run
the race still before me?[10]

I am a sapling
in a grove of ancient oaks,
a passing mention in the annals of creation:
a brief notation,
hid in marginalia.

But these many works of Your hands—
the age-old earth,
the abiding stars—
are young to You:
King of the Ages.
Immortal.
Invisible.
Incorruptible.[11]
Everlasting.[12]
Alpha.
Omega.
Beginning.
End.[13]

Heaven and earth will pass away,
but You will remain[14]—
and from the ashes of this grieving world,
You will make all things new.[15]

Only that which is united with You
will live forever;
only that which has died
will be born again.

10. Heb. 12:1. 11. 1 Tim. 1:17. 12. Ps. 90:2. 13. Rev. 1:8. 14. Matt. 24:35. 15. Rev. 21:5.

PSALM 103

PRAISE UNINHIBITED

Praise uninhibited,
thanks unrestrained,[1]
to You,
my Lord and God.

With all that I am,
I worship all that You are:[2]
Creator.[3]
Sustainer.[4]
Redeemer.[5]
Healer.[6]

When I was dragged down by darkness,
You searched for me,[7]
found me,[8]
set my feet on solid ground,
clothed me in a robe of righteousness,
surrounded me with mercy.

In Your presence,
my soul is refreshed,
renewed,
raised to new heights.[9]

Do You not invite all
who labor and are heavy-laden
to find rest in You?[10]

Friend,[11]
Advocate,[12]
Savior.[13]

1. Ps. 150:1–6. 2. Rom. 12:1. 3. Isa. 40:28. 4. Heb. 1:3. 5. Job 19:25. 6. Exod. 15:26. 7. Ps. 139:1. 8. Luke 15:6, 9. 9. Ps. 16:11. 10. Matt. 11:28. 11. John 15:15. 12. 1 John 2:1. 13. Matt. 1:21.

To the children of Your covenant
You made Yourself known
in law and love,
in earthquake,
fire,
wind—
a compassionate Father,
quick to forgive,
time and again.[14]

Once I walked according to my own ways,
a stranger to mercy—
but now I have been brought near
by the blood of Christ.[15]

Once I was separated from You
by a chasm I could not cross—
but now I sit at Your table,
an heir of endless grace:
wholly loved,
wholly forgiven—
though we are here one moment,
gone the next:
flourishing,
fading,
forgotten.

What am I but dust,[16]
held together by the breath of God?[17]

And yet You call me Your beloved:
a child of the Most High King.

Your love is unending,
unceasing,
untiring,

14. Ps. 130:3–4. 15. Eph. 2:13. 16. Eccles. 3:20. 17. Job 34:14–15.

generation
to generation,[18]
beginning
to end,
for all who walk in the light of Your face,[19]
who delight in Your ways.

You rule and reign over all creation,
over all that lives and breathes:
over every distant star,
over hosts of heaven
that proclaim Your glory,[20]
do Your bidding!

May all that exists
by Your joyful decree
join the eternal song of
praise uninhibited,
thanks unrestrained,
to You,
my Lord and God.

18. Ps. 100:5. 19. Num. 6:24–26. 20. Ps. 19:1.

PSALM 104

CANVAS OF CREATION

Lord God,
with all that is in me
I glorify You today,[1]
for You are worthy of all praise
and glory
and honor.[2]

You reign in grandeur,
swathed in the light of a thousand suns,
a terrifying brightness—
the infinite reaches of space
Your chasmic canvas of creation.

You are Orchestrator of wind and wave,
Symphonist of cloud and flame,
the fabric of reality bending to Your command.

At Your Word,
the world was spoken and spun into being,[3]
anchored by gracious gravity.

When the earth was sick with wickedness,
You filled its canyons with the seas,
pushing mountains into the deep,
into a quiet grave—
until,
in Your mercy,
You lifted the land from its slumber,
the waters receding:
a baptismal rebirth.

1. Ps. 86:12. 2. Rev. 5:12–13. 3. Heb. 11:3.

Now You flood the earth with mercy—
streams of water drawing strength from the ground,
all living things drinking deeply:
Revived.
Restored.
Everywhere, life!
Trees humming with birdsong.
Cloud-flecked skies flinging light across the earth.

Life unstoppable.
Uncontainable.
Flora pushing through the fallow ground—
a vibrant menagerie,
an herbivore's endless feast.

Everywhere,
wonders to be mined,
harvested,
cultivated.

Vines heavy with fruit
to be gathered,
crushed,
strained,
casked,
aged.

Wheat to be plucked,
threshed,
kneaded,
heated,
until mystery does its work.

All that lives
lives by Your provision:
trees drinking from the deep,

blessed to become a blessing,
a fortress of shade and shelter—
from rocky plain
to mountain peak,
bird and beast
are free to roam and rest.

The moon and sun keep watch,
keep time.
Night draws its shade across the earth,
the weary sleep,
the nocturnal wake.
(Even in the darkness, You provide.)
Day brings
light and laughter
and toil
until twilight comes.

I am in awe of Your works, God.
The earth is full of the knowledge of the Lord:[4]
the depths of the ocean,
filled with creatures we will never see;
a hidden world of marvels,
strange and numerous,
swirling beneath the vessels of human design.

No living thing can live without Your breath.
You are the Giver of all good things,[5]
the Provider and Sustainer
of all that lives and moves and breathes.[6]

All life is Yours.
All death is Yours.
If I am with You,
will I not live?

4. Hab. 2:14. 5. James 1:17. 6. Acts 17:28.

Apart from You,
will I not die?[7]

Be praised by all these works of Your hands, Lord.[8]
Proclaim that they are very good![9]
All creation bows before You.[10]

Though Your enemies flourish for a time,
soon they will pass away.
But I will rejoice
that I am one with You
in life and death.

May I be a living sacrifice,
holy and acceptable to You, O Lord,[11]
my joy and song.

7. Job 34:14–15. 8. Ps. 143:5. 9. Gen. 1:31. 10. Ps. 66:4. 11. Rom. 12:1.

PSALM 105

GOD OF THE STORY

Father God,
all praise,
glory,
honor,
thanks,
joy
to You,[1]
God of the Story.

The works of Your hand
and heart
are on our lips;
Your Gospel
sounded,
spoken,
spun:

Creation.
Fall.
Atonement.
Denouement.

For who You are,
for who we are in You,[2]
we give thanks!

For Your many mercies,
countless blessings,
we give thanks!

1. Ps. 66:4. 2. Eph. 2:10.

My heart rehearses
the movements of Your grace:
Your work,
wonder,
wisdom,
revealed
in human history.

I am strengthened
as I seek You,
comforted
as I find You—
one with all the faithful before me:
descendants of grace,
children of the covenant.[3]

All praise,
glory,
honor,
thanks,
joy
to You,
God of the Story.

Creation.
Fall.
Atonement.
Denouement.

Mercy
meets
justice
meets
love

3. Eph. 2:12–13.

meets
faithfulness:
death to life,
slavery to freedom,
salvation for the world You love.[4]

I remember
Abraham,
Sarah,
Isaac,
Rebekah,
Jacob,
Rachel—
those who marked out land
with blood,
sweat,
tears[5]—
who contended for Your promises.

I remember Your people:
desert-wandering,[6]
spirit-wandering[7]—
endlessly struggling
to find rest in Your arms.[8]

When the nations found them,
corrupted them,
threatened to sever them
from Your presence,
You fought on their behalf.

I remember Joseph—
left for dead,
rescued,
tested,

4. John 3:16. 5. Heb. 11:1–40. 6. Ps. 107:4. 7. Ps. 119:10. 8. Jer. 6:16.

promoted,
blessed
to be a blessing.

Israel in Egypt.
Egypt in Israel.
Idols in every generation.
Pharaohs in every age.

A thorn in the side of their oppressors,
Your people were followed by prosperity;[9]
strength surrounded them
even in their bondage.

I remember Moses,
Aaron,
Miriam;[10]
Your miraculous deliverance:
the signs,
wonders,
judgments
of Your hand;
trumpet of death,
triumph of life.

Your people
went out with rejoicing,[11]
plundering their captors:
arrayed in jewels,[12]
clothed in the favor of God.

You led them
with swirling cloud
and pillared fire,[13]
fed them with food from heaven;
opened fountains in the wilderness[14]—

9. Jer. 29:11. 10. Exod. 14:1–15:21. 11. Isa. 55:12. 12. Exod. 12:35–36. 13. Exod. 13:21–22. 14. Neh. 9:15.

for You are
Faithful Father.
Keeper of Promises.[15]

To love is to obey;[16]
to live is to dwell
in the presence of the Lord,[17]
God of the Story.

Be blessed!
Be praised!

Creation.
Fall.
Atonement.
Denouement.
Glory!

15. 2 Cor. 1:20. 16. John 14:15. 17. Ps. 23:6.

PSALM 106

COUNTED AMONG THEM

Father,
be praised for Your goodness,
Your faithfulness,
Your endless mercies,
Your awesome works.

Blessed are those who seek Your kingdom,[1]
who walk in the way of life:
who do justice,
love kindness,
walk humbly with You.[2]

May I be counted among them—
a fellow citizen with the saints,
member of the household of God,[3]
child of the Most High King—
though I am a sinner,
descended from sinners:
bent with brokenness,
heartsick,
wayward.

Have mercy on me, Lord.

When Your people suffered in Egypt,
You delivered them from bondage:
a miraculous liberation,
signs and wonders proclaiming Your power—
only for them to doubt Your goodness,
to grumble in their thirst,
when You are the wellspring of life.[4]

1. Matt. 6:33. 2. Mic. 6:8. 3. Eph. 2:19. 4. John 4:13–14.

Have I not been guilty of the same?
Forgive me, Lord.

In their faithlessness,
You remained faithful—
You folded back the waters of the sea
to make a path through the deep.
At Your Word,
the breakers crashed upon
Pharaoh and his army;
they were utterly consumed.[5]

Your dull-hearted people praised You.
At the spectacle of Your power,
they believed.
(Blessed are those who have not seen
and yet have believed.)[6]

No sooner had their faith flourished
than it withered.
Again they groaned.
Again they rebelled,
longing for the comforts
of bondage,
remembering fondly
the land of enslavement.

Your hand provided—
they ate
and ate
and were full—
but their hunger was a curse,
their fullness was starvation;
they brought a plague upon themselves.

5. Exod. 14:1–31. 6. John 20:29.

Have I not been guilty of the same?
Forgive me, Lord.

At every turn,
they turned from You,
bringing judgment upon themselves:
some were swallowed by the earth,
some consumed by fire,
some drank the dust of the idols they worshiped.[7]

Many became forgetful.
Many became complacent.
Many abandoned the Way.

Though they deserved to die,
Your servant Moses intervened,
pleading for mercy.

Likewise has Christ intervened for me.

You gave generously;
they remained thankless.
You prophesied peace;
they remained faithless.
They grumbled against You,
provoking destruction,
courting despair,
forfeiting the blessings
You longed to lavish upon them.

They turned from the Living God
to the company of demons,
from light to darkness,
freedom to bondage,
suffering the consequences of their rebellion.

7. Exod. 32:20.

If not for Your servant Phinehas,
mediator for the people,
none would have survived.[8]

Likewise has Christ mediated for me.

Ever-longing,
never sated,
though water flowed from rock,
bread from heaven,
their rancor festered;
even their leaders succumbed to bitterness.

Though they were called to be
holy,
set apart,
a people for Your own possession,[9]
they lusted after lesser gods,
followed the ways of godless nations,
desecrated the land of Your promise
with the blood of the innocent.

You turned Your face from them,
delivering them over to darkness,
captivity,
despair—
the same story,
told again and again.

Have I not been guilty of the same?
Forgive me, Lord.

In their distress,
their gods could not save,
their lies could not comfort.
They called to You,

8. Num. 25:6–13. 9. Exod. 19:5.

and Your Spirit returned to them.
You cast their sins behind Your back;[10]
You broke the chains that bound them—
all because of Your infinite kindness,
Your limitless mercy.

Likewise has Christ shown mercy to me.

Not all who wander are lost, Lord.[11]
Bring them back—
to the comfort of Your arms,
the joy of Your presence,
the hope of New Creation.

Do You not rejoice
when we repent?[12]
Do You not stand with open arms,
singing us home?

Be praised for Your goodness,
Your faithfulness,
Your endless mercies,
Your awesome works.

You are the God of Second Chances.

10. Mic. 7:19. 11. From J. R. R. Tolkien, *The Fellowship of the Ring* (New York: Ballantine Books, 1965), 213. 12. Luke 15:7.

PSALM 107

GOD OF ZION

Lord,
I speak a grateful blessing
for enduring love,
sustaining grace,[1]
time redeemed,
sorrow lifted.

Thank You,
God of Zion.

You have found us
in our wandering:
shepherded us,
gathered us,
guided us home
from distant lands.

The merciless desert,[2]
scored by wandering feet,
lives to tell of Your kindness:
of mercy for the sojourner,
provision for the hungry.[3]

Thank You,
God of Zion.

The valley of shadow,[4]
home to suffering saints,
lives to tell of Your intervention:
of bonds broken,
freedom given.

1. Eph. 2:8–9. 2. Isa. 35:1–2. 3. Ps. 107:9. 4. Ps. 23:4.

Though we have danced with death,
wedded ourselves to wickedness,
You have rescued us from ruin,
delivered us from destruction.

Thank You,
God of Zion.

The raging sea,[5]
hurler of hearts and hulls,
lives to tell of Your power:
of churning waves,
sinking vessels,
anguished prayers,
calmed swells,
parted clouds,
safe harbor.

We are drowning souls, all—
You have lifted us from chaos,
set us on solid ground.[6]

Thank You,
God of Zion.

Yet we have been
a channel dried up,
an orchard withered to dust:
a godless,
lifeless
wasteland.

In Your faithfulness,
You have revived us,
replanted us—
that we might become

5. Mark 4:35–41. 6. Ps. 40:2.

a thriving,
flourishing
people[7]—
a dwelling place
for the humble,
the meek,
the pure in heart.[8]

The proud will be broken,
the lowly exalted—
such is the way
of the Kingdom of Heaven.

Thank You,
God of Zion—
for Your wisdom,
Your love,
Your mercy,
Your life.

7. Isa. 61:3. 8. Matt. 5:8.

PSALM 108

SPECTACLE OF PRAISE

Father God,
orient me to Your truth today,
that I may be
wholehearted,
single-minded,
uncompromising
in pursuing Your Way.

I pour out my praise before You,
praise to wake the day[1]—
streams of living water
from the deepest wells within me,[2]
unending thanks for all You have done,
happiness doubled by wonder.[3]

I will not hold back my worship
in the sight of a watching world.
I will be a spectacle of praise,
a grateful debtor to grace,
ready at every turn
to make defense for the hope that flames within me.[4]

Flood the world with Your presence, Lord.
Let it be a cup running over,
a temple of glory for all to see.
Creation groans.
Your people yearn.
Come, Lord Jesus.[5]
Deliver us from this darkness.

1. Ps. 57:8. 2. John 7:38. 3. From G. K. Chesterton, *A Short History of England* (New York: John Lane, 1917), 72. 4. 1 Pet. 3:15. 5. Rev. 22:20.

Have You not given us all things?
Life.
Death.
Present.
Future.

Still, I am homesick,
a sojourner with no place to call my own,
a citizen of the City of the Not Yet.

Sometimes it feels as though You have forgotten us;
withdrawn Your Spirit from us,
left us to fend for ourselves.

We have no hope apart from You,
no chance of victory
or flourishing.

Only by Your hand
will we prevail.
Only by Your death
and resurrection breath
will we rise.[6]

6. John 6:40.

PSALM 109

RISE TO MY DEFENSE

Come, Lord!
Rise to my defense.[1]

I am surrounded by wickedness,
hemmed in by hatred,
a chorus of curses.

Evil trails me,
darkness encircles me—
my shame exposed,
my fears named.

The world I knew
has turned against me.

May the evil that afflicts me,
the enemies that plague me,
be utterly condemned,
consumed,
cast off:
a ruinous reckoning,
a back-breaking,
soul-crushing
defeat.

May their names be forgotten,
their habitations abandoned,
their wealth dissipated,
their sin unveiled,
their greed unmasked.

1. Ps. 82:3.

May they sink into the cesspit
of their own depravity,
with only their tortured minds
to keep them company.

Come, Lord!
Rise to my defense.

My head hangs heavy
with sleeplessness and sorrow;
my heart is plagued with fear and worry.
I waste away while evil gloats.

Cut them down where they stand, Lord;
dismantle them
while You build me up
stronger than before—
for You delight in showing me mercy.[2]

With a full heart
I sing Your praise[3]—
that everyone would hear of
Your saving hand,
merciful pardon,
abundant grace.[4]

You are the Guardian of My Soul:[5]
my Defender,
my Deliverer.

Amen.

2. Mic. 7:18. 3. Deut. 6:5. 4. 2 Cor. 12:9. 5. 1 Pet. 2:25.

PSALM 110

ADONAI

Father,
I thank You that You have exalted Jesus,
that He might reign over all thrones,
dominions,
rulers,
authorities,
in heaven
and on earth[1]—
though He came in the form of a servant[2]
and had no beauty or majesty.[3]
He waited to see the salvation of His God,
that He might claim His rightful throne
and be called King,
Victor,
Adonai.

The Gospel of His grace
has gone out through all the earth.
All will bow before Him
and call Him Lord.[4]

Blessed are those who clothe themselves in Your holiness,[5]
for in You is the eternal dawn,
world without end:[6]
the dead raised,
death undone,
creation set free from its bondage.[7]

1. Col. 1:16; Heb. 1:13. 2. Phil. 2:7. 3. Isa. 53:2. 4. Phil. 2:10. 5. Rom. 13:14. 6. Eph. 3:21; derived from the *Gloria Patri* (*Glory Be to the Father*) doxology of liturgical tradition. 7. Rom. 8:21.

Christ,
our King and Priest:[8]
Forever reigning.
Forever interceding.[9]

At Your judgment,
the kings of the earth will fall prostrate,
Your enemies will flee before You,
all will lay down their arms
on the great and terrifying day of the Lord,[10]
when the works of humankind
are laid bare.[11]

On that day,
death will die,
and the children of God
will walk with You
in the cool of the day.[12]

8. Heb. 4:14–16. 9. Rom. 8:34. 10. Acts 2:20. 11. 2 Pet. 3:10. 12. Gen. 3:8–9.

PSALM 111

WORLD OF WONDER

Father,
as dawn breaks,[1]
gratitude stirs within me.

I wake in a world without end[2]—
creation a temple of the Living God.

All Your children cry, "Holy!"

The work of Your hands
is an unbroken hallelujah:
joy incarnate,
mercy manifest
in all You have made.[3]

Labyrinthine beauty.
Infinite artistry—
from the depths of the earth
to the heights of heaven,
all that exists by Your proclamation
declares Your glory.

I wake in a world of
wonder upon wonder,
life coursing through every vein,
mercy and grace woven into every thread.

All that we need
You have provided:[4]

1. Ps. 57:8. 2. Derived from the *Gloria Patri* (*Glory Be to the Father*) doxology of liturgical tradition. 3. Rom. 1:20. 4. Inspired by a line in the hymn "Great Is Thy Faithfulness" (1923) by Thomas O. Chisholm.

blessing upon blessing—
freely given,
freely received.[5]

To the redeemed
You have revealed Yourself in
power,
faithfulness,
justice,
love.

Grace
upon grace!

Revelation
upon revelation!

You have given us all things:
life,
death,
present,
future—
all is ours,
for we are Yours.[6]

Your
works,
words,
wisdom
are
tried,
true,
timeless,
immovable,
unchangeable.

5. Matt. 10:8. 6. 1 Cor. 3:22–23.

Once I walked in darkness,
but in Your mercy,
I was blinded by Your light,[7]
woke with new sight—
all thanks to the God who is
the Resurrection
and the Life.[8]

Now I wake in Your Word-shaped world,
my heart a fountain of praise
to You:
Wonderful Counselor,
Everlasting Father,
Prince of Peace.[9]

Amen!

7. Acts 22:11. 8. John 11:25. 9. Isa. 9:6.

PSALM 112

THE REWARD OF THOSE WHO SEEK YOU

Lord,
be glorified in me today.
You are the reward of all who seek You,[1]
the prize of the humble heart.
Abundant joy
follows those who follow You.
They lack no good thing.[2]

May I walk in faithfulness before You,
that generations after me would call upon Your name.

I am a vine in Your keeping:
florid,
flourishing,
enduring
by Your provision,
Your protection.

When night falls heavy around me,
Your light shines in the darkness;
the darkness has not overcome it.[3]

Anything good in me
is the result of Your goodness.
I extend grace
because You have extended grace to me.
I offer mercy
because You have offered mercy to me.

1. Isa. 55:6. 2. Ps. 34:10. 3. John 1:5.

I strive for holiness
because You are holy.
Generosity,
because You are generous.
Justice,
because You are just.

Those who love You
are steadfast,[4]
their strength ever renewing,[5]
their faithfulness proof of Your faithfulness.

I do not have to fear
heartache,
disappointment,
adversity,
for You will have the last word,
and when all is said and done,
all will be well.[6]

No act of kindness will be forgotten.
No selfless deed will be unremembered.[7]

Though we are hated for Your name's sake[8]—
cursed,
condemned
by those who worship wickedness
and mock righteousness,
their world passes away,
along with its desires—
whoever does Your will
abides forever.[9]

4. Ps. 57:7. 5. Isa. 40:29–31. 6. Inspired by the line, "I will make all things well; and you will see yourself that every kind of thing will be well." Julian of Norwich, *Showings*, trans. Edmund Colledge and James Walsh (New York: Paulist Press, 1978), 229. 7. Matt. 26:13. 8. Rom. 8:36. 9. 1 John 2:17.

PSALM 113

LORD OF LIFE

Sing aloud,
all children of the King;
worship the Lord of Life![1]

Bless the One
whose fire fills the sky,
morning to evening,
the horizon limned with glory.

Worship the Lord of Life!

You are glorious,
high and lifted up,[2]
enthroned above creation,[3]
nothing hidden from Your sight,
all laid bare before You.[4]

Worship the Lord of Life!

You shower blessings
on the broken,
extend mercy to the needy,
seating them in places of honor[5]—
for theirs is the kingdom of heaven.[6]

At Your touch,
the fruitless womb
becomes fertile ground;
weeping gives way
to rejoicing.[7]

1. Rom. 14:8–9. 2. Isa. 6:1. 3. Isa. 40:21–22. 4. Heb. 4:13. 5. Luke 14:7–11. 6. Matt. 5:3. 7. Ps. 126:5.

Sing aloud,
all children of the King;
worship the Lord of Life!

PSALM 114

OUT OF SLAVERY

Lord God,
You know I have spent time in bondage,
a slave to darkness,
bound to all manner of unworthy things.

But in Your mercy,
You have led me out of slavery[1]
into a land of promise,
a place of belonging,
with roots in fertile soil.[2]

At every turn
You have gone before me,
carving paths through sea and sand,
stemming time and tide,
that You might lead me home.

At Your Word,
creation trembles;[3]
nature bends to Your command.
The earth and the heavens groan,
longing for the blessed not-yet.

Who is like You, Lord,
who makes a way in the wilderness;
rivers in the desert?[4]
Who blots out our transgressions
and remembers them no more?[5]

1. Rom. 6:17–18. 2. Ps. 1:3. 3. Ps. 96:7–9. 4. Isa. 43:19. 5. Isa. 43:25.

PSALM 115

GATHER UP THE PRAISE

Father,
to Your name
be all honor;
to You
be all acclaim![1]

Gather up the praise
of this bustling world:
creation thriving,
humanity flourishing,
galaxies expanding—
praise!

Though our hearts are fickle,[2]
our tongues loose,[3]
though we hoard glory for ourselves—
may we learn to look to You,
King of Glory,
He who is deserving of all praise.[4]

The earth is a temple
desecrated by idols
made in our image,
in our likeness—
saddled with
our blindness,
our deafness,
our speechlessness,
our powerlessness.[5]

1. Ps. 89:15. 2. Jer. 17:9. 3. Prov. 18:21. 4. Ps. 145:3. 5. Hab. 2:18–20.

In Your mercy,
give us the strength to turn
from comforting lies,
from the illusion of control;
to fall upon Your kindness—
for You alone are God,
the One to whom all will give account.[6]

By Your grace,
You prepare a place for us
in the House of the Father,[7]
where the poor,
the crippled,
the blind,
the lame
are honored guests
at the table of the King.[8]

You pour out blessings upon us—
full measure,
cup overflowing:
the favor of God
on the children of God.

You, who are high and lifted up,[9]
have given us dominion over the earth,
put the hope of eternity in our hearts[10]—
for You are not God of the dead,
but of the living.[11]

While breath is in my lungs,
I will join the song of the redeemed:
to Your name
be all honor;
to You
be all acclaim!

6. Heb. 4:13. 7. John 14:2–3. 8. Luke 14:21–23. 9. Isa. 57:15. 10. Eccles. 3:11. 11. Mark 12:27.

PSALM 116

FINISHED WORK

Lord,
how can I express my love for You?
You have covered me with Your kindness.
Ransomed me with Your blood.[1]
Revealed Your heart to me.
Called me Your own.[2]

I have walked with one foot in the grave,
seduced by sin,
dragged down by death,
beaten within an inch of my life—
but at the sound of my groaning,
You lifted me from darkness.[3]

Though I was undeserving of Your mercy,
You saved me according to Your righteousness;
restored me according to Your faithfulness—
for Your heart is with the humble[4]
and the poor in spirit.[5]

Though I am an unfinished work,[6]
I rest in Your finished work.[7]

In You,
I am a New Creation,[8]
spared from the mouth of the grave,
saved from a life of futility,
of endless wandering.

1. Eph. 1:7. 2. Isa. 43:1. 3. Luke 1:79. 4. James 4:6. 5. Matt. 5:3. 6. Phil. 1:6. 7. John 19:30. 8. 2 Cor. 5:17.

Buried with Christ,
raised with Christ,
I walk in newness of life.[9]

When I abandoned all hope in human fellowship,
in the safety of friends,
You worked Your will
in the midst of betrayal.

How can I thank You for all You have done?
No sacrifice,
offering,
vow
would be enough.
I am indebted to You,
with no way to settle my accounts.

There is nothing for me to do
but receive Your grace,[10]
magnify Your name,
declare Your goodness
for all who will hear.

When my days come to an end,
receive my spirit—
for it is a holy thing to die in the arms of God.

You were with me at my birth[11]
and in the generations before me.
You have covered me with Your kindness;
rescued me from ruin.

What can I do but love You,
honor You,
walk with You?

9. Rom. 6:4. 10. Eph. 2:8. 11. Ps. 139:13–16.

I have nothing to offer but grateful praise,
to join in song with the children of Your covenant,
to sing the glories of Your grace.[12]

12. Eph. 1:6.

PSALM 117

BE PRAISED!

With
heart,
mind,
body,
soul,
I praise the Lord of Earth,[1]
King of Heaven,[2]
Master of worlds
seen
and unseen.[3]

Be praised, Lord!

May all lands,
peoples,
tongues—
all who live
and breathe—
praise You
for Your infinite love,[4]
profligate mercy,
abiding promises,[5]
everlasting faithfulness!

Be praised, Lord!

1. Ps. 66:4. 2. 2 Chron. 20:6. 3. Inspired by the words of the Nicene Creed. 4. Rom. 8:39. 5. 2 Pet. 1:4.

PSALM 118

YOUR KINDNESS HAS NO END

Father,
my heart overflows with thanksgiving,[1]
my soul is grateful beyond measure—
for I am loved by You,
kept by You,
anchored by You.

Your kindness has no end.

With all the people of God I proclaim
the infinite riches of Your goodness.
With every daughter,
every son—
every indwelled temple of Your Spirit[2]
I proclaim,
Your kindness has no end!

In my despair,
You have been my hope.
In my bondage,
You have been my freedom.[3]

Every anguished prayer,
bitter tear,
sleepless night,
has been seen by You,
known by You—
my Comforter,

1. Ps. 23:5. 2. Rom. 8:11. 3. 2 Cor. 3:17.

my Ransomer,
my Righteousness.

Though I have had my share of consolations—
a warm bed,
a hearty meal,
the fellowship of friends—
all have been momentary pleasures,
pleasant inns along the road home to You.[4]

When the Enemy assaults me,
be the strength of my heart.[5]
When darkness plagues me,
be the wind at my back.
When I am lost in a godless land,
be the light on my path,[6]
guiding me to rest.

Your presence is my
verve,
vigor,
rhythm,
rhyme—
my soul's sole saving grace.

May our homes
be filled with Your presence.
May the talk of our tables
be Your Story,
Your Gospel,
Your Grace:
the nourishment of our hearts—
for You made us for Yourself,
and when we fell into sin and darkness,[7]

4. C. S. Lewis, *The Problem of Pain* (1940; repr., New York: Macmillan, 1962), 115. 5. Ps. 73:26. 6. Ps. 119:105. 7. Episcopal Church, *The Book of Common Prayer and Administration of the Sacraments and Other Rites and Ceremonies of the Church* (New York: Oxford University Press, 1990), 362.

You came among us,
the Word of God made flesh,[8]
to bear the burden of our trespasses,
to descend into the darkness of the grave
and ascend in glory,
loosening the bonds of death,
raising us to new life.[9]

I have died with You.[10]
I will rise with You.[11]
I abide in You.[12]
I will reign with You.
Even when I am faithless,
You remain faithful.[13]

In Your mercy,
You have flung wide the gates of salvation,
that I may enter freely
as a citizen of Your Holy City.

That which was barred to me
has been opened through the gift of
Your body and blood[14]—
a curtain torn in two,[15]
that Your Spirit might dwell
in a broken vessel such as me.

Hallelujah!
Your kindness has no end!

Lord Christ,
You had no beauty or majesty.
You were scorned and rejected[16]—
You,
around whom all history turns,
all reality orbits.

8. John 1:14. 9. Rom. 6:4. 10. Rom. 6:8. 11. 1 Thess. 4:16. 12. John 15:4–5. 13. 2 Tim. 2:11–13. 14. Heb. 10:19–22. 15. Matt. 27:51. 16. Isa. 53:2–3.

You have chosen the foolish things in the world
to shame the wise,
the weak things of the world
to shame the strong.[17]

At the rising of the sun,
I will lift my voice in song[18]—
for all creation testifies to Your goodness.[19]

May Your mercy go before me this day, O Lord.
Bless the words of my mouth,
the work of my hands.[20]
Lead me in the way of salvation.[21]

All who are called by Your name
and walk in Your might
bear the blessing of Your hand.
What is our worship
if not simple thanks for all You have done?

Once we walked in darkness,[22]
the blind following the blind.
But now,
because of Your abundant grace,[23]
we walk in the light of a new dawn,
awaiting the brightness of full day.[24]

May my life be a living sacrifice—
holy,
consecrated,
freely given.[25]

Be praised, Lord—
for there is none like You.[26]

17. 1 Cor. 1:27. 18. Ps. 57:8. 19. Rom. 1:20. 20. Deut. 28:12. 21. Ps. 25:4–5. 22. Isa. 9:2. 23. John 1:16. 24. Prov. 4:18. 25. Rom. 12:1. 26. Ps. 86:8.

Your power,
glory,
goodness
is unrivaled,
unmatched,
unapproachable.

Your kindness has no end!

PSALM 119

THE WORD, THE WISDOM, OF GOD

I will not forget
the Word,[1]
the Wisdom,[2]
of God:
Light to My Feet,[3]
Lamp to My Way—
Faithful Guide,
Counsel for the Journey Home.[4]

Path

Keep me, Lord,
on the narrow way of Christ:[5]
the path that leads to life.[6]

To walk with You
in spirit,
in truth,[7]
is my deepest desire—
to be wholehearted,
single-minded,
eyes fixed on Jesus:[8]
Living Word,[9]
my Daily Bread.[10]

For Your commands are my delight.[11]
In Your presence,
I am never forsaken.[12]

1. John 1:1. 2. Prov. 8:1–9:12. 3. John 1:5. 4. Ps. 16:7. 5. Matt. 7:14; John 14:6. 6. Ps. 16:11; Prov. 10:17. 7. John 4:24. 8. Heb. 12:1–2. 9. John 1:14. 10. John 6:35; Job 23:12. 11. Ps. 1:2. 12. Ps. 37:25.

Abundance

The life I long for—
life of abundance,
promise,
blessing—
is found in the keeping of Your Word,
the purity of heart and mind.[13]

Your promises
keep me from stumbling;
Your love
saves me from the pull of lesser things.

May I live
humbly,
justly,
mercifully
before You,[14]
filled with new songs[15]
to voice the glories of Your grace.

Guide

Abundant Spirit,[16]
Cheerful Giver of Life,[17]
surround me today,[18]
help me stay the course.

With open eyes,
may I discover greater wonders still,
as I venture deeper
into the heart of God.

May I make the most of the time given to me,[19]
this brief sojourn—

13. Matt. 5:8. 14. Mic. 6:8. 15. Ps. 40:3. 16. Joel 2:28. 17. John 10:10; see the Nicene Creed: "We believe in the Holy Spirit, the Lord, the Giver of Life." 18. Ps. 139:5. 19. Ps. 103:13–18.

living,
dying,
hoping,
dreaming—
walking in Your wisdom,
grounded by Your grace.

While those around me
stagger in darkness,
walking the paths of the dead,[20]
may I remain steadfast, Lord.

Shield me from their hatred.
Spare me from their ridicule.

May all sin in me
be uprooted;
all pride purged.

In the midst of trial,
when the world turns against me,
I will cling to Your promises,
rest in Your faithfulness.

Lead me, Lord;
Your Word,
my lamp.

Freedom

I am drawn downward,
to the dust from which I came,[21]
lifted only by Your
Wind and Word—
restored
by the breath[22]
of Your Spirit.

20. Prov. 14:12. 21. Gen. 2:7. 22. John 20:22.

In the night of my despair,
You fill me with fresh strength,
renewed hope,
patient trust—
that I might resist
the shame that taunts me,
the lies that haunt me.

I turn my eyes from empty things,
my heart from lesser loves—
and find in You again
beauty,
mercy,
kindness,
delight.[23]

Your grace is a garden, unrestrained,
wide and wild,
bountiful,
boundless.
The further I venture,
the more I find.

May my heart make
more room for You still.

Understanding

May I be slow to speak,
quick to listen to
all You would say to me.

I am ready to hear, Lord,
to comprehend,
to obey[24]—
to drink deeply from the water of life.[25]

23. Ps. 37:4. 24. Luke 11:28. 25. John 7:37–38.

Stay before me,
my Guiding Light,
along this winding path—
Your presence my joy,[26]
Your truth my delight.

Yet my heart still leans away,
drawn to ephemeral light,
to passing pleasures,
surrogate saviors.

Draw me back, Lord,
into the safety of Your keeping.

Affirm what You have promised to me:
that I am Your beloved,
raised from death to life,
Your holy workmanship,[27]
created in Christ Jesus
to advance the kingdom of God.

Give me a desire for holiness,
a joy in obedience.

Affection

May I be rooted and grounded
in Your Love,[28]
secure in Your salvation—
that I may be ready to make a defense
for the hope within me.[29]

May Your Word
find fertile soil in my heart—
growing,
producing,
multiplying.[30]

26. Ps. 4:6–7. 27. Eph. 2:9–10. 28. Eph. 3:17–19. 29. 1 Pet. 3:15. 30. Mark 4:8.

May I keep to Your path:
secure in Your affection,
faithful to Your calling.

Give me a voice
to proclaim Your truth
in the presence of the strong,
in halls of power,
in places of privilege.

Your Living Word
is my joy,
my prize;
Your Abiding Truth
my melody,
my meditation.

Presence

Consider, Lord,
the words of Your promise:
"All will be made new."[31]

Is this not the hope of my life?

In the midst of pain,
suffering,
heartache,
I take comfort in the knowledge
that this affliction will one day
give way to glory.

Though the curses of the proud cut deep,
my roots run deeper still,
firm in the fertile soil of Your Word:
my comfort,
my confidence.

31. Rev. 21:5; Isa. 43:19.

My anger burns against those who
turn from Your truth,
scorn Your commands,
live to themselves.

In my pilgrimage,
You have walked with me;
Your love a song in the night;
Your presence the reward of my devotion.

Promise

Where else would I go, Lord,
when You have the words of life?[32]

There is no other shelter,
no other haven.

I will walk in
Your Will,
Your Wisdom,
Your Peace,
Your Promise,
all the days of my life.[33]

Your favor is the reward of my faithfulness.

As dusk falls,
I take account of the day—
my thoughts,
actions,
intentions,
temptations,
hesitations.

May I be quick to follow You, Lord,
quick to repent,
quick to obey.

32. John 6:68. 33. Prov. 2:6–8.

When all hell chases me,
when darkness stalks me,
give me the strength to remember
who I am,
who You are,
who I am in You.

As night grows heavy about me,
I am drawn to worship,
Your Spirit moving over my
restless thoughts,
waking dreams.

Surround me with
the fellowship of the saints;
all who love You
fear You,
follow You—
whose words can be trusted,[34]
whose counsel leads to victory.[35]

As the earth is filled with the knowledge
of the glory of the Lord,[36]
may I be filled to overflowing.

Trust

You have been good to me,
faithful in all Your promises—
though I am still learning wisdom,
still growing in grace,
still being shaped into the image of Christ.[37]

There was a time
when I was indifferent
to Your Way,[38]
when I was more prone

34. Prov. 27:6. 35. Prov. 15:22. 36. Isa. 11:9. 37. Rom. 8:29. 38. John 14:6.

to wandering[39]
than belonging.

But Your goodness ruined me;
Your mercy spoiled me.

Every day,
I see others turn from You.
I endure their falsehoods,
their half-truths,
their curses.

But I will remain
faithful,
hopeful,
worshipful,
counting it all joy
when I suffer
trial,
hardship,
affliction
for Your name.[40]

Clay

I am not
self-existent,
self-sufficient,
self-sustaining;
I am clay in Your hands,
brought to life by Your breath,[41]
nourished by Your Word.[42]

Though I am taunted by empty promises,
lured by lust and sin,
my eyes are fixed on You, Lord:[43]
the source of all my hope.[44]

39. Inspired by a line from the hymn "Come, Thou Fount of Every Blessing" (1758) by Robert Robinson. 40. James 1:2. 41. Gen. 2:7. 42. John 6:63. 43. Heb. 12:1–2. 44. Ps. 39:7.

Pain rouses me,
turns me back to You,
breaks me open
to be filled with a peace,
love,
mercy
that transcends understanding.[45]

May I be a living witness
to all around me,
friends and foes alike:
a testimony to the kindness of God,
who has called me to holiness,
righteousness,
faithfulness.

Longing

I wake to longing,[46]
desperate for the water of life,
for the well that will not run dry[47]—
for redemption,
renewal,
fulfillment.

When, Lord?
When will all these things come to pass?

I am stretched
to the end of my strength;
is there yet more room for suffering?

I hold to Your promise—
that I will live to see Your goodness,
that those who judge me
will themselves be judged;
with the measure they use,

45. Phil. 4:7. 46. Ps. 63:1. 47. John 4:13–14.

it will be measured back to them.[48]

In the midst of oppression,
I hold to the covenant of Your love.
In this web of lies,
I cling to Your truth.[49]

Though I am a hair's breadth from death,
I will remain faithful.

Raise me up, Lord!
Give me a new song to sing.[50]

Grace

Heaven and earth will pass away,
but Your Word will not pass away.[51]

For those with eyes to see,
the work of Your hands proclaims
Your presence,[52]
Your kindness,
Your mercy,
Your invitation.[53]

Creation exists by Your decree,
flourishes for Your glory.

Though I am constantly given over to death,[54]
Your Word is Life to me.[55]

I am the beloved of God[56]—
sustained by Your grace,
strengthened by Your provision,
shielded from darkness
by the might of Your hand.

48. Matt. 7:2. 49. John 8:32. 50. Ps. 40:3. 51. Matt. 24:35. 52. Rom. 1:19–20. 53. Matt. 11:28. 54. 2 Cor. 4:11. 55. John 17:17. 56. Col. 3:12.

No amount of religious fervor
could earn Your favor;
no sacrifice
could gain Your approval.[57]

Your grace is a wide-open space.[58]

Sweetness

Your Word,
Your truth,
is the love of my heart,
the reflection of my mind,
the strength of my countenance
in the presence of the wicked.

Though I am a student,
Your instruction has given me
understanding beyond
the wisdom of this world.[59]

May the so-called sages of this age
stand in awe of the insight
obtained by fear of You.[60]

In the power of Your Spirit,
I resist evil,
hold to Your truth,
remain at Your side
on the path that leads to Life.[61]

I found Your words
and I ate them.
They became my joy,
my heart's delight.[62]

57. Ps. 40:6. 58. Ps. 18:19. 59. 1 Cor. 3:19. 60. Prov. 9:10. 61. Ps. 16:11. 62. Jer. 15:16.

In following You,
my vision is clear,
my mind unclouded.

May every weight
and ensnaring sin
be laid aside
as I run the race set before me,
looking to You,
the author and perfecter
of my faith.[63]

Lamp

Your wisdom
illumines the path before me:[64]
leads me on,
leads me home.

May my commitment be firm,
my will unwavering.

In my weakness,
may I lean on Your strength.[65]

May the power that raised Christ from the dead
give life to my mortal body.[66]

I bless You as
You teach me,
praise You as
You guide me.

Though death pursues me,
I rest secure in the care of
the Living Word.

63. Heb. 12:1–2. 64. Ps. 16:11. 65. 2 Cor. 12:10. 66. Rom. 8:11.

Those who doubt You
are like waves of the sea,
driven and tossed by the wind[67]—
but I hide beneath the shadow of Your wings,[68]
safe in Your keeping,
anchored by Your promises.

Love
May darkness scatter.
May my path be unhindered
as I walk in Your Way.[69]

Evil encroaches,
but I must be about my Father's business.[70]

When I do not have the strength to stand,
bear me up, Lord—
that I may live to see Your promises fulfilled,
to know my hope
was not false hope.

Those who reject You
will be rejected;
those who curse You
will be cursed—
while those who fear You
walk in the light of Your love.

Righteousness
I have sought to do Your will—
my gaze fixed upon You,
not turning to the left or the right.[71]

Will You,
who sees in secret,
not reward me?[72]

67. James 1:6. 68. Ps. 91:4. 69. Matt. 7:13–14. 70. Luke 2:49.
71. Prov. 4:25–27. 72. Matt. 6:4.

Save me from the grip of evil.

May I be found faithful,
righteous,
above reproach,
secure in Your love,
a teachable spirit within me,
a worker with no need to be ashamed,
rightly handling the word of truth.[73]

Save me from the tyranny of the wicked.

Rise up, Lord—
banish evil;
break the yoke of oppression.

Your wisdom is precious,
Your righteousness priceless—
more than riches,[74]
fame,
glory.

I have nothing but contempt
for those who trade Life for Death.

Wonder

I have wondered at the unseen
workings of Your Spirit within me,
the quiet grace of sanctification,
the slow flourishing of wisdom.

I am desperate for Your presence,
parched for the Water of Life.[75]

How often have You shown grace to me?
Extended mercy to me?

73. 2 Tim. 2:15. 74. Prov. 8:11. 75. Rev. 22:17.

We love
because You first loved us.[76]

Deliver me from temptation, Lord.[77]
Though evil baits me,
may I resist it.
Though sin crouches at my door,
may I subdue it.[78]

Turn Your face upon me.
Fill me with Your Spirit.

I weep for those who know Your way
but do not keep it;
who have seen Your light[79]
but choose to walk in darkness.

Zeal

I love Your Word,
Your Wisdom.

I am enraptured
by Your goodness,
Your mercy.

In a world that has forsaken You,
I burn with passion for Your truth.

Though I am poor and needy,[80]
I am loved by You,
discipled by You.

Your Word is
just,
steady,

76. 1 John 4:19. 77. Matt. 6:13. 78. Gen. 4:7. 79. Heb. 6:4–6. 80. Ps. 40:17.

tried,
true.[81]

When I am plagued by
pain,
fear,[82]
worry,
hardship,
Your promises speak Life to me.
Your truth seeds Joy in me.

Dawn

In the light of dawn,
I raise my voice to You.[83]
With all that is in me,
I cry for mercy;
You are my only hope.

May I be a living witness
to Your saving hand—
for You are God not of the dead
but of the living.[84]

When night falls,
Your words comfort me:
In time,
justice will be done.
Mourning will give way to dancing.
Weeping to rejoicing.
In time,
the lawless,
graceless,
merciless
will be defeated.

81. John 17:17. 82. 1 John 4:18. 83. Ps. 108:2. 84. Mark 12:27.

As I wait,
I worship—
grateful for Your nearness,
Your goodness,
Your abiding truth.

Deliverance

I carry overwhelming grief,
crippling sadness—
but I am not destroyed.[85]

Your Word will not return void;
it will prosper;[86]
it will bring me peace—
for You are able to save to the uttermost
those who draw near in Christ.[87]

Do You not intercede for me?[88]
Intervene for me?
Interpose Your blood for me?

All who seek You
find You;[89]
All who fall from You
will fall by You.

Though all the world turn away,
I will draw closer still.[90]

Here I stand:
a child of mercy,
grounded in
Your Word,
Your Wisdom,
Your truth everlasting.

85. 2 Cor. 4:8–9. 86. Isa. 55:11. 87. Heb. 7:25. 88. Rom. 8:26. 89. Matt. 6:33. 90. James 4:8.

Power

Power is a persecutor in prideful hands—
but I have resolved to bow
only to You,
give allegiance
only to You:
King of kings.[91]

Your kingdom is like
treasure buried in a field.
Like a pearl of great value.[92]
I have staked everything
on the beauty of Your Gospel.

May I abhor evil,
hold fast to what is good.[93]

May my days be
governed by praise,
my nights blessed with peace.[94]

May I delight to do Your will
in my inmost being,[95]
to walk in all Your ways—
for nothing is hidden from You.[96]

Belonging

When I lift my voice to You,
You hear me.[97]
When I ask for understanding,
You fill me.[98]
When I cry for deliverance,
You find me.[99]

I praise You,
Living Word.

91. Rev. 19:16. 92. Matt 13:44–45. 93. Rom. 12:9. 94. Ps. 4:8. 95. Ps. 51:6. 96. Heb. 4:13. 97. Ps. 17:6. 98. Col. 1:9. 99. Ps. 32:7.

Ancient Wisdom.
Everlasting Joy.

I praise You,
for my soul dwells secure;
my feet have ceased their wandering.

Your
Word and Wisdom
are my blessing,
my bearing,
my peace,
my prize.

I am often lost
but always found.
Often wrong
but always righted.
Often weak
but always strengthened
by Your Spirit in me.[100]

I will not forget
the Word,
the Wisdom,
of God:
Light to My Feet,
Lamp to My Way—
Faithful Guide,
Counsel for the Journey Home.

Keep me, Lord,
on the narrow way of Christ:[101]
the path that leads to life.[102]

To walk with You
in spirit,

100. Eph. 3:16. 101. Matt. 7:14; John 14:6. 102. Ps. 16:11; Prov. 10:17.

in truth,[103]
is my deepest desire—
to be wholehearted,
single-minded,
eyes fixed on Jesus:[104]
Living Word,[105]
my Daily Bread.[106]

For Your commands are my delight.[107]
In Your presence,
I am never forsaken.[108]

Amen.

103. John 4:24. 104. Heb. 12:1–2. 105. John 1:14. 106. John 6:35; Job 23:12. 107. Ps. 1:2. 108. Ps. 37:25.

PSALM 120

SACRED BENEDICTION

Father,
You are the God who sees,
who hears,
who acts—
a present help in time of need.[1]

My prayers do not go unanswered,
my longings unsatisfied,
my wounds unhealed.

But I dwell in a world of curses.

Everywhere I turn,
I am greeted with sacrilege,
casual blasphemy,
vacuous knowledge,
empty wisdom.

When will we learn that life and death
are in the power of the tongue?[2]
That every holy word uttered
is an invocation,
a sacred benediction,
in harmony with Your eternal song?

I am a stranger here—
a citizen of heaven
in a colony of hell.[3]

1. Ps. 46:1. 2. Prov. 18:21; James 3:5–12. 3. 1 Pet. 2:11.

Give me the strength, Lord,
to sow peace where there is violence,[4]
mercy where there is judgment,
life where there is death.
Amen.

4. Inspired by the Prayer of Saint Francis.

PSALM 121

KEEPER OF MY SOUL

Lord,
though fear assails me,
You have not left me as an orphan in this world.[1]

I hear Your song in the cool of the dawn,
in the heat of the day,
in the waning twilight hours.

Every hill is limned with the light of Your presence.
Every tree bends to the wind of Your Spirit.[2]

May my eyes behold You:
Helper.
Creator.
Sustainer.
Defender.

You brood over my waking and sleeping,
my toil and rest.

Wherever I go,
I remain in the hands of God:
secure in Your safekeeping.[3]

Keeper of My Soul,
when shame and sorrow
hang heavy about me,
when the day becomes too much to bear,
when the quiet of the night
makes room for lying voices—
shelter me in Your presence.[4]

1. John 14:18. 2. John 3:8. 3. Ps. 139:1–6. 4. Rev. 7:15.

When darkness assails me,
when sin plagues me,
be merciful, Lord.

May my feet be steady,
my heart steadfast.[5]

Keep me.
Sustain me.

May my eyes behold You, Lord:
Helper.
Creator.
Sustainer.
Defender.

5. Ps. 57:7.

PSALM 122

COMING KINGDOM

Father God,
when Your people gather—
the children of the King
united in worship
and wonder—
we are filled with the fullness of Your joy.[1]

We have tasted
and seen
Your goodness,[2]
walked in the light
of Your radiance,[3]
glimpsed the coming kingdom
in the here and now.

New Jerusalem,
Heaven's Holy City,
whose gates are never shut—
the nations will walk by your light;
the kings of the earth will bring their glory and honor
to you.[4]

Mountain city
of gold and glass
and every precious stone,
inscribed with the names of the prophets
and apostles—
there will be no temple in you,
for the Lord God
and the Lamb

1. Ps. 16:11. 2. Ps. 34:8. 3. Isa. 60:1–3. 4. Isa. 60:11; Rev. 21:25.

will rule
and reign forever.

There will be no sun,
nor moon,
for the glory of the Lord
will illumine
and enlighten you.[5]

You will be called
Place of New Beginnings,
for the old things will be forgotten
when all is made new.[6]

As we long for that day,
may we walk in unity
and in peace.[7]
May Your Spirit
guard us from every temptation,
every influence of evil,
within and without,
that You may present us—
broken vessels all—
blameless
before You.[8]
Amen.

5. Rev. 21:10–26. 6. Rev. 21:4. 7. Eph. 4:3. 8. Col. 1:22.

PSALM 123

WHEN I SEE YOU

When I see You, Lord,
see You as You truly are:
sovereign,
faithful,
kind,
merciful,
just,
I am filled anew with
faith,
hope,
and love.[1]

Have mercy on me, Lord;
turn Your face upon me.[2]
Spare me from
mockery,
ridicule,
derision,
from all that mocks You
and the children of Your covenant.

Beauty instead of ashes,
I pray,
the oil of gladness instead of mourning,
a garment of praise
instead of the spirit of heaviness.[3]
Amen.

1. 1 Cor. 13:13. 2. Ps. 27:9. 3. Isa. 61:3.

PSALM 124

WHERE WOULD I BE?

Lord,
where would I be without
Your faithfulness,
Your providence,
Your grace?

If not for Your guiding hand,
I would be lost in this world—
a wanderer in the dark,
prey for every enemy of the light.

In Your mercy,
You have sheltered me,[1]
defended me,
delivered me.

I will rejoice—
for I have been brought from death to life,[2]
pain to joy,
bondage to freedom!

Only by Your saving hand
do I live to tell the tale.
Amen
and amen.

1. Ps. 91:1–2. 2. John 5:24.

PSALM 125

WOMB OF THE SPIRIT

I rest in the womb of the Spirit—
shielded,
surrounded,
by the
Giver of Life.[1]

Slowly,
incrementally,
You knit me together[2]—
trust forming in embryo,[3]
hope coursing through nascent veins,
as I am made in Your image,[4]
formed to Your likeness.[5]

You encompass
the children of God:
a nurturing sanctum[6]
about us,
a safe haven,
a forever fortress.

The powers of this age beckon—
bent to blind me,
bind me,
lead me astray.

But You are the wall about me:[7]
Faithful Defender,
Generous Giver

1. Inspired by the Nicene Creed: "We believe in the Holy Spirit, the Lord, the Giver of Life." 2. Ps. 139:13. 3. Ps. 51:6. 4. Gen. 1:27. 5. Rom. 8:29. 6. Isa. 44:2–5. 7. Ps. 3:3.

to all who seek first Your kingdom
and Your righteousness.[8]

Those who seek their own way,
who turn from the path of life,
will march into the mouth of the grave—
while the beloved of God
find rest in Your presence.[9]

Amen.

8. Matt. 6:33. 9. Heb. 4:9–10.

PSALM 126

UNCONTAINABLE JOY

Father,
You know—
more than any other—
that I have lived with
unfulfilled longings,
unsatiated desires,
dormant dreams.

By the miracle of mercy,
in timing known by You alone,
You gave me my heart's desire[1]—
not by my effort or striving,
but on account of Your relentless kindness to me.[2]

To be given such a gift
by such a Giver
felt too good to be true.
To know that my hope
was not false hope,
that my faith
was not wishful thinking,
that my yearning
was not in vain,
but all was
seeded by You,
seen by You,
nurtured by You,
known by You—
filled me with an uncontainable joy;[3]
an infectious hallelujah.

1. Ps. 37:4. 2. Eph. 2:7. 3. 1 Pet. 1:8.

When others ask,
what brought this thing about? I say,
"The Lord has done great things for me."[4]

Now, Father,
do the same for all Your suffering servants;
all who live in poverty
and in chains,
heavy beneath the weight of human dominion,
the mind's delusion,
who long for life abundant,[5]
a future and a hope.[6]
Renew them.
Refresh them.
Bring them to the land of promise.

In Your mercy,
their mourning will turn to dancing.[7]
The fallow fields will burst forth with life!
Rivers will carve paths through the desert.[8]
Dry bones will grow sinew and flesh.[9]
Everlasting joy will be upon their heads.
Sorrow and sighing will flee.[10]
Amen.

4. Luke 1:49. 5. John 10:10. 6. Jer. 29:11. 7. Ps. 30:11. 8. Isa. 43:19. 9. Ezek. 37:6. 10. Isa. 35:10.

PSALM 127

LORD OF THIS HOUSE

Who is our head and host?

Christ,
Lord of the Feast.

Who watches over us?

Christ,
our stronghold and refuge.

Who grants us peace?

Christ,
our Eternal Sabbath.

Who is the giver of life?

Christ,
in whom all the families of the earth are blessed.[1]

Who is King over this house?

Christ,
who loved us
and gave Himself up for us[2]—
who calls us His own.

1. Gen. 12:3. 2. Eph. 5:2.

PSALM 128

THE WAY OF BLESSING

Lord,
what a backward,
twisted world this is—
where power is weighed by wealth,
influence by arrogance,
permanence by prominence.
True blessing is found in the laying down of arms:
full-scale surrender to Your grace,
a headlong dive into the mystery of Christ.[1]

To follow You,
to know You,
is Life;
to love You
is to lean into reality:
to swim downstream,
tread downhill,
run unhindered.

Your commands
are freedoms.
Your discipline
is kindness.[2]

In light of Your grace,
everything is a blessing.

Does Your life
not animate all that we do?
Is it not the lifeblood of every family—
a living, breathing

1. Rom. 16:25–27. 2. Heb. 12:5–11.

tapestry of tendriled roots
and branching leaves?
The subsonic song humming beneath
our daily chores,
our careless words,
our casual curses?

May we remember that we are Yours.
That You are with us.[3]
That we are with You.[4]

May we walk in Your ways,
know the power of Your resurrection,
share in Your sufferings[5]—
that all our comings and goings
would be blessed,
that every thought and intention of our hearts
would be blessed,
that our fathers and mothers
would be blessed,
that our daughters and sons
would be blessed,
our work blessed,
our leisure blessed,
our worship blessed,
our mourning blessed,
our rising blessed,
our striving blessed,
our resting blessed—
blessing
upon
blessing
upon
blessing.
Amen.

3. Matt. 1:23. 4. John 15:4–5. 5. Phil. 3:10.

PSALM 129

I HAVE CONFIDENCE

I have confidence in this:
You who began a good work in me
will bring it to completion in Your good time.[1]

For as long as I can remember,
the enemies of my spirit
have sought to
steal,
kill,
destroy.[2]

I will overcome by the blood of the Lamb
and the word of my testimony.[3]

Though I am scored by suffering:
furrowed,
upturned,
exposed—
You seed new life in me.

In Your mercy,
You have routed darkness,
broken the chains that bound me,
led me to a place of abundance.[4]

Those who mock Your rule,
scorn Your kingdom,
forfeit life.
They waste away—
power sapped,

1. Phil. 1:6. 2. John 10:10. 3. Rev. 12:11. 4. Ps. 66:12.

hubris humbled,
blessings relinquished.

As for me,
I have confidence in this:
You who began a good work in me
will bring it to completion in Your good time.

PSALM 130

THE WORD OF YOUR PROMISE

Father,
I am so deep
in the depths
of the dark,
so pressed down,
covered over,
long-forgotten,
that sun
and sky
and light
and laughter
seem like nothing more
than a dim dream.

But could it be
that even here
my cries do not fall on deaf ears?
That even in this quiet grave,
You are—
somehow—
with me?

If not for Your mercy,
Your gracious forgetfulness,
I would have no ground for hope,
no expectation of deliverance.

You have proven Yourself to be
Savior.

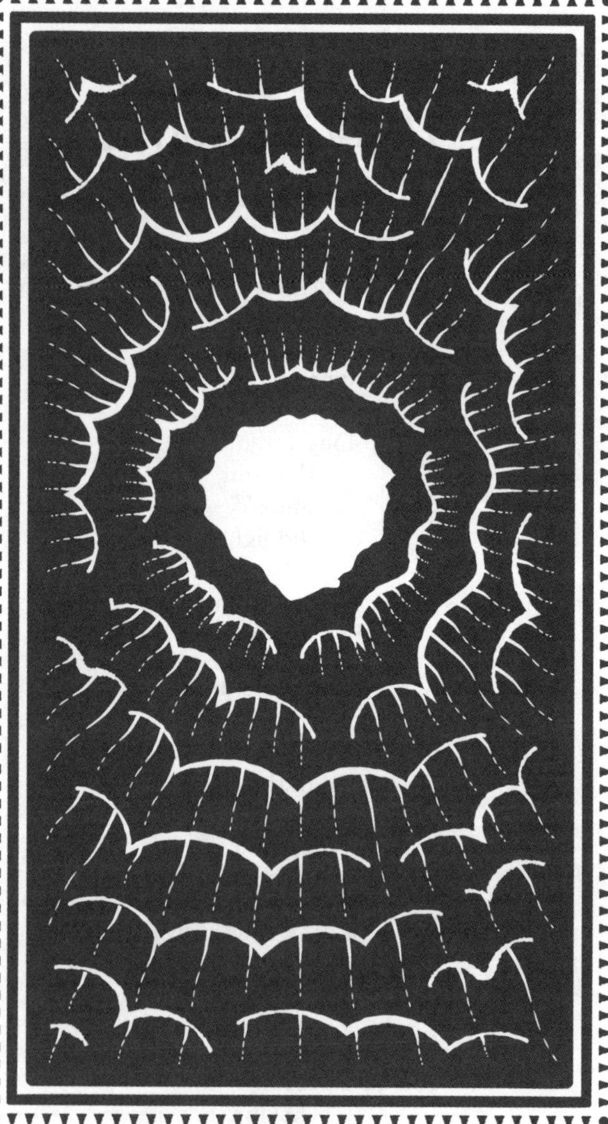

Deliverer.
Lifter of the Weak.

I trust
that in Your good timing
I will rise from this death,
that the promises You have spoken
will come to pass,
that this broken earth,
scarred by affliction,
will birth life—
sevenfold,
a hundredfold.

I quiet my soul.[1]
I breathe in the Word of Your promise.
I wait,
I trust,
that the night
will yield to the dawn.

Is this not what You ask of us, Lord?
To hope,
in spite of unspeakable grief,
debilitating sorrow,
impenetrable darkness,
that somehow,
impossibly,
this broken world
will one day shake free
from the bonds of death?
That the former things
will pass away?[2]

How?
When?

1. Ps. 131:2. 2. Rev. 21:4.

To that unreasonable end—
that irrational redemption—
I lift my voice with the redeemed and say,
*"Come, Lord Jesus!
Come soon."*[3]
Amen.

3. Rev. 22:20.

PSALM 131

IN YOUR ARMS

Father,
I rest in Your arms—
spirit humbled,
heart comforted.

Here
in the solace of Your presence
I cease my restless longing,
my endless striving.

There is nothing for me
to prove,
to do—
no effort,
no struggle.

I am a child
cradled in embrace,
held in the grasp of love.

Hope rises in me,
as it does for all who know
the comfort of Your arms.[1]

1. Deut. 33:27.

PSALM 132

YOUR SERVANT DAVID

Father,
may I be like Your servant David,
who suffered for his righteousness,
wept for his faithlessness,
who desired
above all
to give You praise,
to build a place of worship,
a habitation for Your glory.
Though he lacked for nothing,
he was restless
for the house of the Lord.

He foresaw a time
when many would come from east and west
to feast at Your table,[1]
to gather with all the saints
and sing the glories
of Your grace—
a day when the earth would
become the temple of the Lord,
when all the people of God
would wash their robes
in the blood of the Lamb.[2]

Did You not promise
that from the stem of Jesse
a shoot would spring forth?[3]
That the Spirit of the Lord
would rest upon Him?[4]

1. Matt. 8:11. 2. Rev. 7:14. 3. Isa. 11:1. 4. Isa. 11:2.

That righteousness and faithfulness
would be the belt about His waist?[5]
That at His coming
the wolf would dwell with the lamb;
the leopard with the young goat?[6]
That His throne would have no end?[7]

Father,
in Your mercy
You have chosen a people
to be filled with Your Spirit,
that we might be a kingdom of priests;[8]
a holy nation:
children of the New Creation.

In You,
we lack no good thing[9]—
for we are kept by Your love,
clothed in Your righteousness.[10]

Father,
may I be like Your servant,
who longed for a day he would not see
in the land of the living,
when the Word[11]—
Root of David,
Lion of the tribe of Judah[12]—
would be made flesh,
and the earth would behold His glory,
the glory as of the only begotten Son of the Father,
full of grace and truth.[13]
Amen.

5. Isa. 11:5. 6. Isa. 11:6. 7. Heb. 1:8. 8. Rev. 1:6. 9. Ps. 34:10. 10. Isa. 61:10. 11. John 1:1–5. 12. Rev. 5:5. 13. John 1:14.

PSALM 133

SO VERY GOOD

Father,
it is so very good
when unity prevails
where bitterness once held sway.

It is so very good
when the oil of humility
anoints those gathered in Your name.

It is so very good
when sister,
brother,
mother,
father,
find common ground,[1]
when our fellowship is blessed
by the peace of Your Spirit.[2]

Amen.

1. John 17:22–23. 2. Eph. 4:1–6.

PSALM 134

A PRAYER FOR THOSE IN MINISTRY

Lord God,
I pray for all who live to
serve and shepherd Your people:
all overseers,
deacons,
elders,
priests,
rectors,
pastors,
ministers—
may they love You
with a whole heart,
an undivided will.[1]

May they love Your Church well,
their families well,
their friends well—
and so honor You.

Be near to them, Lord.[2]
Bless the work of their hands.
In Your holy name I pray,
Amen.

1. Ps. 86:11. 2. James 4:8.

PSALM 135

LORD OF PRAISE

Lord of Praise,
be praised by all
who love and serve You!

May I join in their song,
swept up in the splendor of holiness,[1]
lifting hands and heart[2]
to magnify Your name.[3]

May worship be my first language,
gratitude my native tongue—
for Your goodness and mercy
have ransomed me from the grave,
filled me with uncontainable joy.[4]

Lord of all lords,
You are not distant from us,
hiding behind the curtain of creation;
You have tabernacled among us,[5]
revealed Yourself in word and wonder,
called us to belong to the family of God.[6]

Subdue our idols.
Conquer our imaginations.
Do what is in Your heart to do:
muster wind and wave,
height and depth,
thunder and lightning,
to accomplish Your will.[7]

1. Ps. 96:9. 2. Ps. 134:2. 3. Ps. 34:3. 4. 1 Pet. 1:8. 5. John 1:14. 6. Rom. 1:6. 7. Matt. 6:10.

When You intervene,
slaves are freed,[8]
wonders are made manifest,
death is defeated,
empires are conquered,
the widow is given a home,
the hungry are filled.[9]

You are
Creator.[10]
Abba.[11]
Father.

Savior.[12]
Immanuel.[13]
Son.

Wind.
Fire.[14]
Spirit.

Your name is carried forward
through the ages of human history—
civilizations passing into memory,
kingdoms collapsing into dust.

You reign above all,
Your throne from
generation
to generation,[15]
Your face turned toward
the children of Your promise.[16]

The human heart is deceitful above all things,[17]
a temple of idols

8. Luke 4:18. 9. Luke 1:53. 10. Isa. 40:28. 11. Rom. 8:15. 12. Luke 2:11. 13. Matt. 1:23. 14. Acts 2:1–4. 15. Lam. 5:19. 16. Rom. 9:8. 17. Jer. 17:9.

with no power to speak,
to comfort,
to save,
to deliver.[18]

Those who exchange Your glory
for such things,
who trade Your truth for lies,
are given up to impurity,
to the dishonoring of their bodies,
to a debased mind,
to all manner of
unrighteousness,
covetousness,
evil.[19]

But all who call You King,
who worship You in spirit and truth,
who are washed in Your blood,
covered in Your kindness,
praise You!

Lord of Praise,
be praised by all
who love and serve You!

Amen.

18. Isa. 45:20. 19. Rom. 1:22–29.

PSALM 136

GLORY BE

Lord God,
all goodness flows from You:
all holiness,
beauty,
grandeur
is the prism'd light
of the radiance of Your glory.

You are above all things,[1]
and all things are Yours:
thrones,
dominions,
rulers[2]—
for You alone are
King of kings
and
Lord of lords.[3]

Glory be to the Father,
to the Son,
and to the Holy Spirit,
as it was in the beginning,
is now,
and ever shall be,
world without end.[4]

Painter of nebulas,
of clustered stars,
of orbital moons,
of worlds.

1. Ps. 138:2. 2. Eph. 1:21. 3. Rev. 19:16. 4. The *Gloria Patri* (*Glory Be to the Father*) doxology of liturgical tradition.

Symphonist of comets
and constellations,
of supernovas,
of solar flares.

Glory!

Deliverer of Your children;
Defender of Your people;
Faithful Father
to the ransomed
and redeemed.

Evil-vanquisher,
sea-tamer,
wave-splitter,
shepherd,
comforter.

Glory!

No enemy can stand before You,
no power of darkness prevail against You.

All that is godless,
graceless,
hell-bent,
will be exiled,
cast out—
while the meek
will inherit the earth.[5]

Glory!

You are friend to the downcast,
Father of the fatherless,[6]
Savior of the suffering.

5. Matt. 5:5. 6. Ps. 68:5.

In Your mercy,
You send rain on the just
and the unjust alike.[7]

Glory!

Glory be to the Father,
to the Son,
and to the Holy Spirit,
as it was in the beginning,
is now,
and ever shall be,
world without end.

7. Matt. 5:45.

PSALM 137

HEART IN EXILE

Father,
I have sojourned in distant lands,
tasted the bitter salt of my tears[1]
as I longed for Your nearness[2]—
though You seemed as distant
as the leaden sky above.

When my heart is in exile,
guide me home.[3]

My worship withers.
My joy wastes away.
Evil harasses me—
mocking my devotion,
cursing my faithfulness.

I have no songs left to sing,
no prayers to pray—
not in this desolate place,
where all I know is Your absence.

Are You not with me still?
Does Your Spirit not intercede for me
in unutterable groanings?[4]
Though I do not see You,
give me the strength to believe.
Fill me with inexpressible joy again![5]

In Your power,
defeat the darkness

1. Ps. 42:3. 2. Isa. 26:9. 3. Isa. 2:2. 4. Rom. 8:26. 5. 1 Pet. 1:8.

that has defeated me.
Utterly consume
the evil that threatens
the children of Your covenant;
that lays siege to Your kingdom.

Draw me back, Lord,
that I might know
the comfort of Your presence once again.

When my heart is in exile,
guide me home.

Amen.

PSALM 138

I CHOOSE YOU

Father God,
I choose You today—
above all idols,
all distractions,
all lesser loves
that contend for my affection.

You alone are
hope of my heart,
light of my eyes,
strength of my days.
I pour out my praise before You.[1]

I walk in the temple of creation,
my feet on holy ground,
as all Your works proclaim[2]
Your goodness and grace.
What name can save but Yours?
What truth abides but Yours?

In the night of my distress,
You speak to me.
In my weakness,
You restore me;
when my courage is sapped,
You fill me with new strength.

I long for the day when the earth
will be filled with Your knowledge;[3]
when all thrones and dominions and powers

1. Ps. 42:4. 2. Ps. 19:1. 3. Hab. 2:14.

lay prostrate before You
and all creation rests.

In that day,
the kingdoms of earth
will be Your kingdoms, Lord,[4]
and the streets will be filled with singing.

You dwell in unapproachable glory[5]
but have made Yourself known
to the humble-hearted:
a God who weeps with us,
rejoices with us,
abides with us.[6]

To the stubborn,
the proud,
the hard-hearted,
You stand at a distance;
a far-off voice;
a half-forgotten dream.

I have known my share of troubles,
afflictions,
hardships,
but You have never left me.[7]
My life is in Your hands.
My days are Yours.

When darkness encroaches,
You comfort me.
When evil assails,
You fight for me.[8]

Abide with me, Lord,
as I abide in You,[9]

4. Rev. 11:15. 5. 1 Tim. 6:16. 6. 1 John 4:12. 7. Heb. 13:5. 8. Josh. 23:10. 9. John 15:4.

and the mystery of Your will is revealed:
the plans You had for me
before time began.[10]
Amen.

10. Jer. 29:11.

PSALM 139

KNOWN BY YOU

Lord,
may I take comfort in the knowledge
that I am known by You.[1]

My
rest,
rising,
ruminations,
are known by You.

My
direction
and digressions
are known by You.

My pondering
and pontificating
are known by You.

I am
encircled,
enveloped,
embraced,[2]
lost in wonder
at the thought that I am
loved by You,[3]
seen by You.

You are with me in my wandering,
my hiding,

1. John 10:14–15. 2. Ps. 32:7. 3. Rom. 8:38–39.

my fear,
my denial.[4]

You follow me to the ends of the earth,
the deepest hell,
the highest heaven,
the gates of paradise,
the paths of the dead.

You find me on the dawn's horizon,
in the sea's watery grave.

When I am lost in darkness,
when my sight fails me,
I am led by Your unseen hand.

If You are with me,
what can stand against me?[5]
Do You not see all things,
know all things?
Are Your eyes not eyes of fire,
piercing through the deepest dark?

My body was
woven and spun
by the breath of God—
cell upon cell
threaded,
laced,
spirited into being
in the shade of the womb—
Your image imprinted,
Your glory bestowed.

Never have I been a mystery to You;
never have I been less than

4. Gen. 3:8–9. 5. Rom. 8:31.

fully known,
fully loved.

Before my eyes saw light,
You saw me.
Before I learned to keep time,
You peered into my future,
scribed the arc of my life
on the tablet of Your heart.[6]

Is it true that the King of Heaven and Earth
thinks of me?
It is.

How often, Lord?
Too often to number.
Too frequently to count.

Why should I be graced with such an honor?
Because you are My beloved
and I delight to show you mercy.

Are You with me,
every moment of every day?
I am.

Still,
there are those who resist You,
rebuke You,
curse Your kingdom,
mock Your mercy.

I turn my face from them,
wash my hands clean of them—
for there will be a day of reckoning
when all the enemies of God

6. Prov. 7:3.

will reap what they have sown,[7]
while the beloved of God
will enter Your everlasting joy.[8]

Purify my heart.
Cleanse my mind.
Sanctify my soul.
Renew my strength[9]—
as I sojourn on Your path,[10]
safe in the knowledge that I am
known by You.

Amen.

7. Gal. 6:7. 8. Matt. 25:21. 9. Isa. 40:29–31. 10. Ps. 16:11.

PSALM 140

DESECRATED PLACE

Holy Spirit,
keep me from the sway of sin.
I walk in a world of wickedness:
a desecrated place
where evil triumphs
and goodness is mocked.[1]

All around me are lying voices,
spewing curses.
The heart is deceitful above all things,
desperately sick.[2]

Guide me in the way of righteousness
for Your name's sake.[3]

Save me from the influence of the Enemy,
who knows my weaknesses,
plots my downfall—
step by step,
an incremental corruption.
He whispers in the silence of the night,
in hidden shame,
in unfulfilled desire.

Guide my feet, Lord.
Everywhere I turn,
a trap is laid for me.

Beneath these shallow lusts,
my heart longs for You[4]—
my Lord and God.

1. Ps. 74:10. 2. Jer. 17:9. 3. Ps. 23:3. 4. Ps. 84:2.

Arm me with Your righteousness,
shield me by Your grace,
fill me with Your Spirit.
For this darkness
is but a momentary affliction.[5]

In time,
every stronghold will be broken,
every high place cast down,
every idol ground to dust.

For what can stand against You, Lord?
Will evil not,
in the end,
be its own undoing?
Will all that mocks You
and profanes Your name
not pass away
when You make all things new?[6]

But all who call upon Your name will be saved:[7]
the poor in spirit,
the mourning,
the meek,
those who hunger and thirst after righteousness,
the merciful,
the pure in heart,
the peacemakers,
the persecuted—
the kingdom is theirs.[8]
Amen.

5. 2 Cor. 4:17. 6. Rev. 21:5. 7. Rom. 10:13. 8. Matt. 5:1–10.

PSALM 141

ENDLESS STRUGGLE

Lord,
in this endless struggle,
hear me when I speak.
Find the worship in my words,
the sacrifice in my supplications.

Bless the speech of my mouth,
that I may speak life
in a world of curses.

Keep me from evil,[1]
temptation,
the clash of flesh and spirit,
the company of the godless,
the empty pleasures of the wicked.

If I must be wounded,
if a thorn must twist in my side,
let it be from the hand of a friend—
a humbling blow,
a merciful kindness.

In time,
I will rise from this affliction
with a testimony to Your saving hand,
evidence of Your goodness to me.[2]

No amount of pain,
suffering,
death,
will be in vain.

1. Matt. 6:13. 2. Rom. 8:18.

This sorrow will serve its purpose;
this cross will bear a mantle of glory[3]
beyond compare.[4]

I have no hope in passing things;[5]
I look to You alone, Lord:
my Savior,
my Sanctuary.[6]

May the designs of darkness
be its undoing;
may the schemes of the blasphemous
turn back upon them—
while I live to tell
of the merciful hand of God[7]
in the midst of endless struggle.

3. 2 Cor. 4:17. 4. James 1:4. 5. 2 Cor. 5:17. 6. Ps. 91:1. 7. Neh. 9:17.

PSALM 142

A LISTENING EAR

Father God,
in the dark night of the soul,[1]
be near to me.
When my strength is sapped,
my will is weak,
my heart falters,
lay Your hand upon me.[2]

When I weep before You,
spilling all this grief,
bear with me:
patient,
present,
a listening ear.[3]

When I stagger blind,
lost in the labyrinthine dark,
may Your hand guide me.
When I have no will to carry on,
carry me.

Danger looms at every turn.
One false step would be my undoing,
one wrong move, my ruin.
Evil pursues me,
planting its snares,
orchestrating my defeat.

Is every face
the face of an enemy?

1. Inspired by a poem from St. John of the Cross, "Dark Night of the Soul." 2. Ps. 139:5. 3. Ps. 61:1–3.

Every harbor
a prison?
Every greeting
a curse?

Foxes have holes,
birds of the air have nests,
but I have no place to lay my head.[4]

You alone
are my heart's home,
my glorious inheritance.[5]

In sorrow,
comfort me.
In peril,
deliver me.
In bondage,
liberate me.[6]

May I lift my voice
with all the redeemed,
to sing the glories of Your grace—
that God,
in His mercy,
has rescued me from death.
Amen!

4. Matt. 8:20. 5. Eph. 1:18. 6. Gal. 5:1.

PSALM 143

WORD OF COMFORT

Lord God,
hear me now:
an answer is all I seek—
a word of comfort[1]
to tell me I am not alone.[2]

I know full well
the things I have done
and left undone:[3]
my secret shame,
my illicit desire—
but beneath these shallow lusts,
my heart beats for You still.

I am
harried,
helpless,
pressed,
pursued,
short of breath,
heartsick,
wasting away under the shadow of affliction.[4]

But I am not crushed.
Not abandoned.
Not destroyed.[5]
Not yet.

I cling to distant memories of Your presence,
half-remembered stories of Your goodness.

1. 2 Cor. 1:3. 2. Deut. 31:6; Heb. 13:5. 3. Episcopal Church, *The Book of Common Prayer and Administration of the Sacraments and Other Rites and Ceremonies of the Church* (New York: Oxford University Press, 1990), 360. 4. Ps. 73:26; 109:23. 5. 2 Cor. 4:7–10.

I am a desert wanderer:
sun-seared,
bone dry,
desperate for the water of Your Spirit.[6]

Turn Your face upon me again;[7]
give me peace.
Apart from You,
what is there but death?

Wake me
with the song of Your love.[8]

Guide me
in the ways of Your wisdom.[9]

Save me
from every influence of evil.[10]

Hide me
in the shelter of Your arms.[11]

Make me
a disciple of Your truth.[12]

Lead me
on the path of life.[13]

For the sake of Your glory,
save me.[14]

For the honor of Your name,
deliver me.[15]

Out of Your abundant kindness,
redeem me.[16]

Amen.

6. John 7:37–38. 7. Ps. 27:9. 8. Ps. 40:3. 9. Ps. 25:4. 10. Matt. 6:13. 11. Ps. 17:8. 12. John 14:6. 13. Ps. 16:11. 14. Rom. 7:25. 15. Ps. 34:4. 16. Job 19:25.

PSALM 144

FIT FOR THE FIGHT

Father,
as long as truth contends with falsehood,
righteousness with wickedness,
good with evil,
may I be fit for the fight[1]—
armed with Your Spirit,[2]
bolstered by Your faithfulness.

For what have I but You?[3]
You are the ground beneath my feet,
the roof over my head,
the freedom bought for me,
the righteousness imputed to me.

How can I not triumph
if You are with me?[4]

Though I am a small and passing thing,
You have loved me,
delivered me,
raised me to new life,
breathed eternity into me.[5]

Will You not
move heaven and earth
to rescue Your beloved?
At Your Word,
will every valley not be lifted up?
Every mountain and hill be made low?
Will Your glory not be revealed

1. 1 Tim. 6:12. 2. Eph. 6:17. 3. Ps. 73:25. 4. 1 Cor. 15:57. 5. Eccles. 3:11.

when You make straight
a highway through the wilderness?[6]

You are the Shepherd
who leaves the ninety-nine
to seek Your lost one.[7]

Father, come swiftly.
Wrest me from the mouth of darkness.
Disentangle me from the cords of death.
Deliver me from the grip of the damned.

With joy
You will bear me up
and see me safely home.[8]

Your mercy
is the song of my heart,
the melody on my tongue.
You have not left me as an orphan;
You have come to me.[9]

The world does not see You,
but I see You.
Because You live,
I live.[10]

Father, come swiftly.
Wrest me from the mouth of darkness.
Disentangle me from the cords of death.
Deliver me from the grip of the damned.

May all who trust You
walk in ever-increasing
blessing and favor in Your eyes.[11]

6. Isa. 40:3–5. 7. Luke 15:4. 8. Luke 15:5. 9. John 14:18. 10. John 14:18–19. 11. 2 Cor. 3:18.

May all that we touch
thrive and flourish:
our families,
our resources,
our labor,
our rest—
may Your kingdom come,
on earth
as it is in heaven[12]—
for truly we are
Your beloved.[13]

12. Matt. 6:10. 13. Ps. 108:6.

PSALM 145

THE WAY OF MERCY

Father,
I thank You for
Your abundant love
that triumphs over judgment,[1]
Your common grace
that showers blessings on all[2]*—*
Yours is the
way of mercy.

I praise You,
Lord of History,
the God who rules and reigns,
whose name is above all names.[3]

Who can measure Your glory?
Fathom Your grace?

You have entrusted us with Your Story:
handed down
in ink,
breath,
blood—
the majesty revealed in Christ,[4]
the oracles of God
proclaimed by the people of God.[5]

Hear our song of blessing, Lord,
the melody of thanksgiving
resounding from Your ransomed children,
as we proclaim Your Gospel
in all the earth,[6]

1. James 2:13. 2. Matt. 5:45. 3. Phil. 2:9–11. 4. Col. 1:15–20. 5. Rom. 3:2. 6. Mark 16:15.

to every tribe and people,
nation and tongue.[7]

Your kingdom comes.
Your will is done.
On earth as it is in heaven.[8]

Faithful,
kind,
gracious Lord—
in You
the powerless are exalted,
the hungry are satisfied,[9]
hearts are opened,
longing is sated,
desire is fulfilled.[10]

You are just,
gentle,[11]
present—
always unveiling the truth,
liberating the oppressed,
redeeming the righteous,
vanquishing evil.

May all that lives and breathes
worship You[12]
for Your
abundant love
that triumphs over judgment,
Your common grace
that showers blessings on all—
Yours is the
way of mercy.

7. Rev. 7:9. 8. Matt. 6:10. 9. Luke 1:53. 10. Ps. 37:4. 11. Matt. 11:29. 12. Ps. 150:6.

PSALM 146

LAVISH GRACE

Lord,
as long as there is breath in me,
strength in me,
a beating heart within me,
I will sing Your song:[1]
the song of Your relentless faithfulness,
lavish grace,
inexhaustible love.

Why do we waste our praise on flesh and blood,
on idols that cannot save or deliver?
They are a passing mist,
a fleeting vapor.

But You are everlasting,[2]
Unchanging,[3]
Creator of all,
Sustainer of all,[4]
Immanuel[5]—
who mourns with us,
rejoices with us,
bleeds with us.

You are
Liberator,
Emancipator,
Friend of the downcast,
the lonely,
the weak—
the hope of every homeless heart,
the terror of all who stand against You.

1. Col. 3:16. 2. Ps. 41:13. 3. James 1:17. 4. Heb. 1:3. 5. Isa. 7:14.

The kingdoms of this earth will pass away,[6]
but You are King forever,
and Your reign will have no end.[7]
Hallelujah!

6. Matt. 24:35. 7. Luke 1:33.

PSALM 147

MY JOY, MY DELIGHT, MY SONG

Father,
how can I not return
Your kindness
with praise?
Your mercy
with worship?

You are my joy,
my delight,
my song.[1]

I praise You—
for You have called us to be a holy nation,
a kingdom of priests
reigning upon the earth,[2]
hastening the day
when all the ransomed of God
will come from east and west,
north and south—
crowned with joy,
filled with gladness,
and sighing and sorrow will flee away.[3]

I praise You,
for You bore our griefs and sorrows,
were pierced for our transgressions,
crushed for our iniquities,
that by Your stripes

1. Exod. 15:2. 2. Exod. 19:6; 1 Pet. 2:9; Rev. 5:10. 3. Isa. 51:11.

we might be healed,
restored,
reborn.[4]

Are we not known by name,
like all the morning stars that sing for joy?[5]
Are Your thoughts toward us
not more numerous than all the lights in the heavens?[6]

I praise You
for the Word-shaped wonder of Your world:
cellular,
celestial,
molecular,
electrical,
geological,
gravitational,
glory!

I praise You,
for the meek know Your mercy;[7]
wickedness suffers Your wrath.

For all these things and more,
I praise You, Lord!

My joy,
my delight,
my song.

I praise You
for the gifts of Your hand:
rain to wake the flowering field,
sustenance for all that lives and breathes,
provision
upon
provision.[8]

4. Isa. 53:4–5. 5. Job 38:7. 6. Ps. 139:17–18. 7. Matt. 5:5. 8. Gen. 22:14.

All creation testifies to Your goodness,
calls us to Your faithfulness,
directs us to Your hope.

May all who love You
sing the glories of Your name!
May we go out in joy,
be led forth in peace!
May the mountains,
hills,
trees,
join our song![9]

In You
we rest secure.

In You
our families are blessed.

In You
we flourish,
thrive,
are strengthened,
established.[10]

At Your Word,
sleet and snow,
frost and hail,
blanket the earth.

At Your Word,
winter melts into spring;
creation is reborn.

I praise You
for the revelation of Your grace,

9. Isa. 55:12. 10. Prov. 3:23.

the covenant of Your mercy,
the truth of Your Word—
the gift of God
to the people of God.[11]

Father,
how can I not return
Your kindness
with praise?
Your mercy
with worship?

You are my joy,
my delight,
my song.

Amen.

11. Episcopal Church, *The Book of Common Prayer and Administration of the Sacraments and Other Rites and Ceremonies of the Church* (New York: Oxford University Press, 1990), 364.

PSALM 148

ALL IS YOURS

Eternal Father,
Creator and Sustainer of all,[1]
hear the song of creation
giving You praise!

Your name echoes in the far reaches of space,
as all high and holy things
join in the celestial strain:
angels and archangels,
suns and stars,
galaxies and nebulae,
unimaginable wonders
proclaiming Your power and goodness!

You spoke life into darkness;
Your words create worlds.[2]
All that is,
or ever has been,
is the fruit of Your commands.

Be the song of this suffering earth.
From the depths of the seas
to the heights of heaven,
from cephalopod
to cumulonimbus;
hydrozoa
to heliosphere,
nothing is wasted—
all is Yours!

1. Isa. 40:28. 2. Gen. 1:1–31.

I look upon the terra firma of Your design:
the rolling topography of
cavern, plain, peak,
teeming with creatures great and small,
too many to number,
too extravagant to believe.[3]

And reigning over them all,
humankind,
the crown of creation.[4]
From peasant to king,
all bear Your image;
In You,
all the families of the earth are blessed.[5]

May they all,
with one voice,
join the song of creation
and give You praise!

For You are the hope of every heart,
the desire of every nation,[6]
the Savior of all who call upon Your name.[7]

Be glorified, Eternal Father,
for You are worthy of all praise.
Amen.

3. Gen. 1:20–22. 4. Inspired by a conversation with N. T. Wright, Westminster Abbey, spring 2004. 5. Acts 3:25. 6. Hag. 2:7. 7. Rom. 10:13.

PSALM 149

GOSPEL KING

Alleluia!
With all the saints,
I sing Alleluia
to the Gospel King![1]

Rejoice!
With revelry,
refrain,
remembrance,
we rejoice,
lifting our voices to praise
the Gospel King!

Delight!
The Lord delights in His beloved:
all humble-hearted,
grace-grounded
children of the Gospel King!

Glory!
May the godly give You glory!
As we sing ourselves to sleep,
worship as we wake,
arm ourselves with praise,
be glorified,
our Gospel King!

You will bring the world to order,
bring balance to the scales,
establish Yourself as Lord and Sovereign.

1. Luke 4:16–21.

Every knee will bow[2] before the
true,
living,
eternal,
ascended,[3]
returning
Gospel King.

2. Phil. 2:10. 3. Acts 1:6–11.

PSALM 150

SHELTERING MERCY, ENDLESS GRACE

Lord God,
may You be glorified[1]
in every house of worship,
by every heart on sojourn,
every pilgrim,
exile,
son,
daughter,
who calls upon Your name![2]

Be lauded by
billowing cloud,
roaring thunder,
by sun,
moon,
star![3]

Be extolled for
Your power,
Your might,
Your justice,
Your love![4]

May Your fame be
sung,
sounded,
strummed,
thrummed,

1. 2 Thess. 1:11–12. 2. Rom. 10:13. 3. Inspired by a line in the hymn "Great Is Thy Faithfulness" (1923) by Thomas O. Chisholm. 4. Ps. 108:4.

drummed,
hummed![5]

May Your Gospel be
proclaimed in all the earth![6]

May Your glory be declared by all
living, breathing things—
all that is from You,
through You,
to You![7]

Be praised, Lord—
for Your sheltering mercy,[8]
Your endless grace.[9]

Amen
and
amen.

5. Ps. 145:4–7. 6. Matt. 28:18–20. 7. Ps. 69:34. 8. Ps. 91:1–2. 9. John 1:16.

ACKNOWLEDGMENTS

Thank you to Bob Hosack and the team at Brazos Press for their belief in this endeavor. To Eric Salo for editing and finalizing the manuscript. To Carolyn Weber, Trevin Wax, and Dave Schroeder for honest feedback. To Nathan Swann for his beautiful illustrations for both *Sheltering Mercy* and *Endless Grace*. And finally, to our wives, children, and the many friends and family members who have supported us and encouraged us along the way, we are eternally grateful.